THE FAST TRACK GUIDE TO LOSING WEIGHT AND KEEPING IT OFF

Jan Yager has a Ph.D. in sociology from The Graduate Center of The City University of New York (1983), an M.A. in criminal justice from Goddard College, and she did a year of graduate work in art therapy at Hahnemann Medical College.

The author of 45 books, translated into 34 languages, and a professional speaker who leads workshops and delivers keynotes on time management, work relationships and other topics, Dr Yager has taught the "Sociology of Health" at the University of Connecticut, St John's University, and the New York Institute of Technology. She currently teaches sociology and criminology courses in the department of sociology at John Jay College of Criminal Justice/CUNY.

Dr Yager worked as a counselor at a camp for overweight girls when she was seventeen. She has been researching weight issues since at twenty she was hired to write the proposal for a book that rated diets (which went on to become a bestseller). Her books include: *Work Less, Do More: The 14-Day Productivity Makeover; When Friendship Hurts: How To Deal With Friends Who Betray, Abandon, Or Wound You; Friendshifts®: The Power of Friendship and How It Shapes Our Lives; Victims: A Moving Portrait of Crime Victims Including Victims of Homicide, Aggravated Assault, Robbery, Rape, & Burglary; Creative Time Management for the New Millennium: Become More Productive and Still Have Time for Fun; 365 Daily Affirmations for Happiness; 365 Daily Affirmations for Time Management; 365 Daily Affirmations for Healthy and Nurturing Relationships; Road Signs on Life's Journey: Sayings and Insights to Help You Find Your Way; The Pretty One* (a novel)*; Friendgevity* (forthcoming) and others.

She's been interviewed on major talk shows including *The Oprah Winfrey Show, The Today Show, The View, Good Morning America* and *NPR Radio*. To book Dr Yager as a speaker, contact your favorite lecture bureau or e-mail jyager@aol.com. For more information, go to http://www.drjanyager.com

THE FAST TRACK GUIDE TO LOSING WEIGHT AND KEEPING IT OFF

JAN YAGER

RUPA

Published by
Rupa Publications India Pvt. Ltd 2019
7/16, Ansari Road, Daryaganj
New Delhi 110002

Sales centres:
Allahabad Bengaluru Chennai
Hyderabad Jaipur Kathmandu
Kolkata Mumbai

First published in the US and Canada by Hannacroix Creek Books, Inc.
(www.hannacroixcreekbooks.com)

First published in the Indian subcontinent by
Rupa Publications India Pvt. Ltd, 2019.

ISBN: 978-93-5333-722-3

First impression 2019

10 9 8 7 6 5 4 3 2 1

Printed at HT Media Ltd, Gr. Noida

CONTENTS

1

WELCOME TO A FRESH START!

Whether you are in your twenties and this is the first time you're really trying to do something about your excess weight, or you're in your thirties, forties, fifties, or older, and you've been on one or many diets to no avail, *The Fast Track Guide to Losing Weight and Keeping It Off* offers a unique time management approach to this lifetime challenge.

Yes, there are countless books about diet and weight loss, exercise, and even on how to keep off the weight you lose. You may even have read one, ten, or more of those books. So why another one? Because this book offers a different approach to your weight challenge that might just overhaul the way you approach your weight issues. It provides you with proven time management tools and strategies that you can now apply to your weight loss, exercise and maintenance concerns.

The Fast Track Guide to Losing Weight and Keeping It Off may also help you to stop the war you have with food, labeling some foods as "good" and others as "evil," or bemoaning exercise as something that is too time-consuming for you to fit into your already too-demanding schedule.

Ask yourself the following questions:

- Have you ever looked in the mirror and wondered how you could have gained so much weight?
- Have you ever tried to lose weight, and keep it off, but always seem to regain what you lost, plus a few extra pounds?
- Are you so tired of dieting that you've resigned yourself

to being overweight the rest of your life?

- Have you been putting off doing certain things for your job, or your social life, waiting "until I lose the weight"?
- Would you like to do something about your weight, for health reasons, but you've just given up believing it's possible for you to make permanent changes?
- Do you find yourself eating even when you're not hungry?
- Do you have two or more sizes in your wardrobe, but long for being just one, consistent size: the preferred size for your height, body frame and activity level?

If you answered "yes" to even one of the above questions, there is help, and hope, in this book. Read on!

You Need to Believe You Can Lose Weight and Keep It Off

The Fast Track Guide to Losing Weight and Keeping It Off is a motivational book offering a clear "take charge" approach to managing your diet and to maintaining that weight loss rather than going back up the scale once you achieve your ideal weight.

This book could be read to get you motivated to start a healthier weight program or, once you are following a sound program, you could read it as a way of reinforcing your efforts by providing extra encouragement.

Please note these very important caveats: this book is *not* a diet book nor is it meant to be used alone. You are urged to consult with a doctor, nutritionist, or a professional trained in weight issues if you have a weight challenge. You are also expected to follow a healthy diet that enables you to weigh in regularly and to be monitored consistently to make sure that you are losing weight in a healthy way for you and your physical and psychological needs.

You will not find only one diet or maintenance plan advocated in this book. There are two reasons for that. The first one, as just stated, is that this is *not* a diet book, but a motivational guide.

The second is because there are many nutritionally sound weight loss programs that will help you lose weight, and keep it off, as long as you stick to it, and, once you lose the weight, you work at maintaining your weight loss rather than regaining any or all of the weight that you lost.

The key is starting a program, *staying* with it, even if you have an occasional slip, and, once you achieve your weight loss, maintaining that weight. You will need to work at keeping track of what you eat (and how much exercise you do) even once you are at your ideal weight, just as conscientiously as you were at the part of this process when you were losing weight.

I have personally been on a multiplicity of programs over the years, with success in weight loss but less success with keeping it off. This time, I am again participating in Weight Watchers®, and it is definitely working better than ever before. I know that is because not only has Weight Watchers® improved its program, but I've changed as well. My husband, Fred, who also wants to lose weight and keep it off, attends the weekly meetings with me. I am also trying harder to go back to the meetings, even if I had a "bad week" the week before, or if I take a "no weigh in" approach that week, but at least I am recommitting to the long term of weight loss and maintenance rather than quick results that, in the past, led to a "rebound" effect of regaining some or all of the weight that I had lost.

This book has been researched and written to help you to attain your goal of weight loss, using productivity principles based on the proven creative time management principles that aid success at achieving business or personal goals. It also looks at the psychology and sociology behind weight gain and loss, with a discussion of the possible causes of your overeating, bingeing, aversion to exercise, or even your resistance to achieving or sustaining your weight loss goals.

Everyone's weight story is unique, however. I can share insights into what might be holding you back from observations and research, but how it applies in your particular situation is up to you to decide.

Of course *you* are ultimately the one who is in charge of your weight loss and maintenance journey. This book, or any other book or even the program that you choose to follow, are only tools on your journey. How effectively or consistently you use this or any other tool is up to you.

Using Creative Time Management Principles to *Finally* Win Your Battle with Weight

Like so many millions with a weight problem, I have been on various diets and I have lost weight, over the years, from a few pounds to as many as 60 pounds, only to regain it (and usually very soon after losing it).

Why had I failed to maintain those weight losses? As you will read about in the all-important Chapter 14, "Maintaining Your Preferred Weight", I had to finally learn that keeping it off is definitely harder than losing it. But if I did have a relapse and regain some of the weight that was lost, I had to learn how to get back on track *before* I regained some or all of the lost weight, and then some.

I am pleased to be able to report that although I was 200 pounds and a size 16 seven months ago, I am now in the 150s and a size 8—just within 15 pounds of my preferred weight. Even more importantly, however, I have retrained my approach to eating and dieting so that I am closer to conquering my compulsive overeating and bingeing than ever before. I have also taught myself to add exercise to my schedule in a way that is much more consistent and less time-consuming, such as dancing to music in my house or taking a fast-paced walk on my way to appointments.

For a longer discussion of my weight challenges, you can refer to a synopsis of my weight history that follows in About the Author at the back of this book. Now I want to get back to talking about what I've learned on my amazing journey to better self-control and joyful eating that *you* could benefit from.

Why was I succeeding this time? It is because I was approaching my weight challenge with a reliance on these four concepts:

1. A commitment to finding out what was behind my overeating *and* my pattern of regaining weight after I had lost it.
2. The application of proven time management techniques that work so well in business and life to the weight challenge through the eight creative weight management principles I developed.
3. The addition of exercise to my schedule or simply "moving more" in a way that was practical and sustainable.
4. The renewed awareness that "keeping it off" is as hard, or even harder, than losing it in the first place and putting forth the energy, time and new habits to make "maintaining my weight loss" a daily goal.

Furthermore, this time, when I began my renewed commitment to losing the weight and keeping it off last May, I rededicated myself to loving myself, regardless of the fact that I had got back to almost 200 pounds. I decided to embrace my overweight self as an unhealthy condition that I wanted to change for various reasons, but without putting myself down and feeling the self-loathing that I used to associate with being overweight or wearing a size that was much too large for my frame.

I took into my heart and emotionally owned the very first affirmation in my own book, *365 Daily Affirmations for Creative Weight Management*: "I love myself, whatever I weigh and whatever my shape."

The second part of that statement, I realized, is as crucial as the first. Without it, a vicious cycle arises.

- Lose weight—a lot of it
- Even at ideal weight, find fault with shape

- The relentless self-criticism, and perfectionism becomes undoing because
- Turn to food for comfort
- Gain weight again
- Self-criticism continues
- Try to lose weight again

So, this time, by loving myself whatever my weight or shape I knew I would have a better chance at breaking that negative, frustrating, counter-productive and unhealthy cycle.

Another important component of my success this time is that I have been relying on a habit that is serving me well as I continue on my weight loss and maintenance journey: my dedication to keeping track of what I am eating, whether it's on my computer, in my cell phone, in my appointment book, or writing it down in a journal. What's important is the keeping track part; for many of us, writing down everything we eat and drink, including meals and snack, helps, so we keep track.

Now, of course, you might be able to keep track of what you eat in your head and if that works for you, great. But if it is not working for you, try writing down what you eat, and not just your meals: keep track of every snack that you have as well. Certainly you will want to do this within the parameters of whatever weight loss program you are following, so you will see a slow, but steady, and healthy weight loss.

It might also be helpful to you to record:

- your thoughts and feelings related to whenever and whatever you are eating and dieting, especially if you are eating when you are not hungry
- how much water you drink
- how much exercise you do every day
- and any other weight program-related concerns

But, most importantly, you have to monitor and keep track of everything you are eating and drinking, and even when. Every single morsel. At least initially. If you are to get a grip on your weight challenge, you need to know exactly what you eat, how big a portion of it, and even what time you are eating it.

Another component of *The Fast Track Guide to Losing Weight and Keeping It Off* approach is to learn to include exercise in your everyday activities, although if you can get to a gym a couple of times a week or have a formal workout routine, that is recommended as well (as long as you are physically healthy for regular exercise and your physician has approved you for it, if you don't have any kind of medical conditions to be concerned about).

For those who don't have time to formally exercise, there are ways to include exercise in your day. For instance, I now park my car in parking lots and walk further to destinations that I already had planned to visit. (All of us, however, have to be careful, of course, not to place ourselves in jeopardy in terms of safety; I am not advocating taking long walks in unattended parking garages, especially late at night.)

I will walk long distances in Manhattan that, previously, I might have instead opted for taking a bus, subway or cab. I try to take the stairs whenever possible instead of the elevator or escalator—although sometimes if it's just too steep an incline, I will choose the elevator.

If I have a choice for a hotel that I will stay at on a business or family trip, I try to pick one that has an exercise room, especially if it has 24-hour access. If there is an indoor pool, that is even better.

The clear message of *The Fast Track Guide to Losing Weight and Keeping It Off* is that no matter how many times you have tried to take weight off, and keep it off, by applying creative time management principles to the weight challenge, and especially by remembering that it is the "keeping it off" that is definitely the hardest part of your creative weight management journey, you may be able to see the short- and long-term results you have always hoped for. You too can transform your approach to food and exercise.

But this book is based on more than just my own experiences and the concepts I've learned from time management research with its application to the weight challenge. It is also based on research I have been doing into weight as a medical sociologist with a Ph.D. in sociology from The City University of New York Graduate Center, including a pre-doctoral fellowship in medical sociology from the National Science Foundation. Over the years, I have taught medical sociology, including the sociology of weight, at several colleges and universities, including St John's University, the New York Institute of Technology and the University of Connecticut.

Prior to obtaining my Ph.D., I worked as a counselor at a camp for overweight girls in upstate New York the summer of my freshman year at college. After graduation, I did a year of graduate work in art therapy at Hahnemann Medical College, studying the mind, including working with patients in internships at a psychiatric hospital and a home for abused and neglected teens. I have also researched and written articles and authored or co-authored books on health, including two books on sleep, as well as books on food and nutrition topics, including the history of vegetarianism as well as ice cream, lecithin, keeping the brain functioning, living a long and healthy life, and also, a proposal for a book on rating the diets, and ghosting the proposal for a doctor's book on overcoming cancer.

To research this book, in addition to background readings, I conducted original weight research consisting of collecting and analyzing seventy-eight questionnaires from men and women throughout the United States and half a dozen foreign countries including the United Kingdom, Denmark, Taiwan, Germany, Spain, Indonesia and India, as well as selected follow-up phone or in-person interviews. I've actively listened to the examples and anecdotes shared by the dozens of participants and numerous leaders at the Weight Watchers® meetings I've attended in my Connecticut hometown, as well as in Florida, Tennessee, and even London locations.

Thanks for discovering *The Fast Track Guide to Losing Weight and Keeping It Off*! I am so excited to be able to help you on your weight loss and maintenance journey. Whether you have to lose ten, twenty, fifty or one hundred or more pounds, it all starts with a single step, a one pound loss. And even before that, it starts with a commitment to creating a new you, a you that's in control of what you eat, and when you eat. A you that no longer sees chocolate or ice cream as "bad" but as foods that you can, in moderation, include in your program, if you want to. I grew up in a house where I was not allowed to have "treats", so I would hide chocolate bars in my desk drawer. Learning to be in control of what I eat, and when I eat it, and finally enjoying food, including, in moderation, a daily "treat", has been an exciting achievement over the last year as I've reduced from almost 200 pounds to 159, down from a size 16 to a size 8.

Please join me on an exciting time management approach to a weight loss and maintenance journey, a journey that I hope you are beginning with increased optimism and a renewed belief in yourself, as this book puts you on the fast track to healthier eating and living.

I invite you to please visit my website— http://www.drjanyager.com—for more information about my coaching services or about any online or in-person workshops I am offering that you might want to attend.

I also welcome hearing from you as you start and continue your own weight loss and maintenance journey. Here is my e-mail: yagerinquiries2@aol.com. Please also sign up to be one of my Twitter followers http://www.twitter.com/drjanyager

In the next chapter, you will learn the eight principles of

creative weight management that are based on creative time management concepts. So go to the next page, so that you continue on your way to a healthier (and happier) you!

2

THE EIGHT PRINCIPLES OF CREATIVE WEIGHT MANAGEMENT

In my book *Creative Time Management for the New Millennium,* I shared the seven principles of creative time management—principles that I developed based on original interviews, observations, and extensive surveys of hundreds of men and women. Here are those seven productivity principles:

Seven Principles of Creative Time Management

1. ***Be active, not just reactive:*** You have to decide to make things happen for yourself, not just react to situations and the demands of others.
2. ***Set goals:*** Short and long (and longer term) goals are a way to break up a big task into more manageable little steps that result in getting the big job accomplished.
3. ***Prioritize actions:*** Whatever is your #1 concern has to take your time, energy and focus. Being nonchalant about what matters rarely works.
4. ***Keep your focus:*** Yes, starting a goal is key, but "staying the course" is even more challenging.
5. ***Create realistic deadlines:*** Trying to accomplish something "big" overnight will backfire. You need to pace yourself and be realistic about how long something will take.
6. ***D-O I-T N-O-W***

   D = Divide and conquer what you have to do.

   O = Organize your materials, such as the diet plan you will

follow, the foods you will eat, and how you will do it.

I = Ignore interruptions that are annoying distractions.
T = Take the time to learn how to do things yourself.
N = Now, not tomorrow. Don't procrastinate.
O = Opportunity is knocking. Take advantage of opportunities.
W = Watch out for time gobblers. Keep track of and stay in control of how much time you spend on the Internet, reading and sending e-mails, watching TV, or talking on the phone.

7. ***Balance your life:*** Yes, work is important. But becoming a workaholic is usually a sign of someone who is a poor time manager; a burnout is likely. Living a life that balances work and personal time and relationships is key to accomplishments that can be sustained over a long term.

Let's see how those principles can help you with your weight challenge, as I have applied and adapted those creative time management principles to the weight loss, exercise, and preferred weight maintenance challenges.

Eight Principles of Creative Weight Management

1. ***Figure out* why *you're overweight and/or overeating:*** Whether you do self-talk, take self-quizzes, go into therapy, or discuss it with a therapist if you are already in treatment, work on the underlying causes of your overeating.

   In my time management book, *Work Less, Do More,* I share my **ACTION!** plan for accomplishing more. What is the "A" in the action plan? It stands for assess. That is exactly what you need to do to start your weight loss journey with the best chance of success. Assess what got you to this place of being overweight or obese so you have a better chance of dealing with your challenge.

   Ask yourself *why*:

- Are you eating because you're stressed out and you need to find healthier alternatives to deal with your stress?
- Are you using your overeating and being overweight to avoid career or personal challenges because you keep putting off trying to achieve your goals till you lose weight?
- Have you fallen into some bad habits, like overeating and being too sedentary, that you have to break in order to get a better outcome when it comes to your weight situation?

2. ***Prioritize doing something about your weight and eating habits as your #1 concern:*** For most people, losing weight and keeping it off requires definite actions. You have to decide that you are going to do something about your weight challenge.

   You need to *focus* on your weight situation. Decide to take action and *do something* about your weight. You need to direct the time and energy towards dealing with your weight situation to see the positive changes and results that you want. Dealing with your weight situation has to be your emphasis; you need to make this a "healthy obsession".

   Prioritize your weight challenge as a primary goal that you are going to put effort and time into, not something you'll deal with whenever you "get around to it".

   Losing weight and keeping it off has to now be a key *priority* in your daily activities if you are to achieve positive short- and long-term results you want. It is not something you can deal with in a haphazard way. It is too easy to gain weight and too difficult for most individuals to take it off. You need a concerted effort.

3. ***Get a medical check-up and pick a medically sound, supervised plan to follow:*** Start off with a physical with your internist so you can rule out any possible medical causes for your weight problem and to make sure your health is good enough to withstand the challenge of a weight loss and

exercise program. Some thyroid conditions, for example, if untreated, can be linked to a weight gain. Discuss weight loss program options (and exercise) with your physician to find a program that will suit you best.

There are numerous medically sound and supervised diet programs out there from which to choose. There are, of course, many factors that will go into your choice: how much time you have to prepare food; how many people you are cooking for, if any, besides yourself; your budget for buying foods; if you prefer a structured or unstructured program and just general guidelines; if you want to work individually with a nutritionist, an internist, on your own, or participate in one of the many available supervised commercial diet programs available; if you have special dietary needs, and so forth. What is key to remember here, however, is that picking the right diet for yourself is a major decision and one that you should address with the importance that it deserves. But don't overreach either, to the point of using that as an excuse not to make the commitment to starting on this healthier eating and exercising journey.

4. ***Be prepared. Plan, shop and prepare for each meal or snack:*** Put "go grocery shopping" and planning meals for each and every breakfast, lunch, dinner or snack on your "to do" list, right up there with career, relationship or childcare priorities.

   Poor planning often leads to "grabbing" high-calorie snacks, getting too hungry to make better food choices, skipping meals, or preparing the same dishes too often causing boredom that can sabotage your creative weight management efforts.
5. ***Keep track of what you're eating or snacking or drinking every day:*** Especially in the beginning of your weight management program, write down every morsel of food you put into your mouth at meals and for snacks.
6. ***Create more manageable goals, reward yourself as you go***

down the scale, as you lose the next smaller unit of weight of the total you have to lose, such as each 1, 3, 5 or 10 pound loss: This principle is based on the time management principle of dividing a big goal, project, or challenge into smaller, more manageable goals or steps in order to eventually achieve your overall goal.

You didn't put this weight on overnight; you're not going to lose it overnight. Reward yourself as you lose the next smaller unit of weight out of the total you have to lose, such as each loss of a pound or even two-tenths of a pound, no matter how tiny, or as you get into the next smaller size in clothes.

Also reward yourself as you achieve each weight loss milestone, say for each one-, five- or ten-pound loss, rather than waiting until you've lost all the weight.

Take this creative weight management program not just a day at a time; break it down even further and take it a meal or a snack at a time. It will seem less formidable to get through the next meal, or even this one day, than however long it may take you to achieve your overall weight loss goal.

Visualize your weight loss by concretizing your goal with increasingly smaller sizes. This works especially well with pants. For example, I began my weight challenge wearing a size 18 pair of jeans; I kept buying at least the next size or two down of the same exact style to motivate myself to get to that next lower size.

7. ***Include exercise, and non-food stress reducers, such as keeping a journal or meditating, into each day:*** Research on the benefits of regular exercise for losing weight and keeping it off are well documented.

   There are, of course, also other benefits to regularly exercising. Recently, for example, new research has offered evidence that being physically active three to five days a week, even with a fifteen-minute daily walk, could also reduce the risk of developing Alzheimer's disease as well as help to keep the brain healthy, and delay or prevent the incidence of neuro-degenerative diseases of the brain in later years.

Dealing with stress more effectively, so that you are less likely to misuse food as a way to cope when you're stressed out, will also help you with your weight loss and maintenance challenges.

8. ***When you reach your preferred or goal weight, make maintaining your weight loss your new #1 priority and goal:*** If you ever gain even two pounds, go back on a supervised, medically-sounded weight plan until you return to your preferred weight, and go back to following creative weight principles one through seven yet again.

   As you know, losing weight is a big step, but it's just the first giant step. Keeping the weight off requires a reapplication of these principles to the weight maintenance phase of your weight challenge.

   Making a lifetime commitment to daily healthy eating and exercise on a regular basis are positive steps toward a healthier lifestyle. For most people with a weight challenge, there is no such thing as a lifetime cure.

   Watching what you eat and determining why you eat or overeat has to be a daily concern, but without obsessing about it. If you find yourself eating out of control, bingeing or reverting back to food addiction, if necessary, seek professional help.

   Stay in touch with reality by weighing yourself daily and wearing clothes with fitted waists; elastic waists can expand and "hide" a weight gain of as much as 30 or 40 pounds.

In summary, here are the eight principles of creative weight management based on time management concepts:

1. *Figure out* why *you're overweight and/or overeating.*
2. Prioritize *doing something about your weight and eating*

habits as your #1 concern.

3. Get a medical check-up *and pick a medically sound, supervised plan to follow.*
4. Be prepared. *Plan, shop and prepare for each meal or snack.*
5. Keep track *of what you're eating or snacking or drinking every day.*
6. Create more manageable goals, *and reward yourself as you go down the scale, as you lose the next smaller unit of weight of the total you have to lose, such as each 1, 3, 5 or 10 pound loss.*
7. Include exercise, and non-food stress reducers, *such as keeping a journal or meditating, into each day.*
8. *When you reach your preferred or goal weight, make maintaining your weight loss your new #1 priority and goal.*

In the next chapter we'll look at some of the psychological reasons behind the *why* behind your current overweight and/or overeating situation.

3

DEALING WITH THE PSYCHOLOGICAL ASPECTS OF OVEREATING AND WEIGHT CHALLENGES

Creative Weight Management Principle #1:

Figure out why you're overweight and overeating.

It is crucial to understand *why* you overeat, or compulsively eat, even when you are not hungry, so you can effectively manage your weight for the long term. If you fail to understand the *why* behind your overeating, compulsive eating, or bingeing—or even the why behind your overweight situation if you do not overeat, but perhaps in your case you are too sedentary, so you are not burning off the calories you are taking in which is resulting in weight gain—once you lose the weight, the compulsive behavior, or any other habit that is behind your weight challenge, may return and sabotage your efforts, leading to a rebound or yo-yo phenomenon.

Failing to understand, and deal with, the psychological or sociological aspects of overeating or being overweight that may be contributing to your weight problem may even prevent you from losing the weight in the first place.

Here's a challenging concept to consider: the late psychologist David Leeds used to tell me that for some, rejection is actually *easier* to take than acceptance.

This is a key concept to ponder because it means that for some of us, as we approach our goal weight and we're experiencing the acceptance we have always craved, we may pull back towards rejection and return to overeating, which will lead to rejection by us, or by others, instead of going forward towards slimness and acceptance.

Not everyone has complex reasons behind his or her overeating or weight problem. If it is just a matter of bad habits that you have to change—perhaps in your case, just learning better portion control is all that's needed since you are consistently eating too much for your height, frame and level of daily activity—you will have different "issues" than someone for whom eating too much "to fill up emotionally" is behind their overeating.

This chapter is not a substitute for working with a therapist or weight counselor or coach on the underlying motives to your weight problem. It is just a general overview of some of the psychological or sociological causes that might be behind your overeating or weight problems. Hopefully you may find some or all of the ideas in this chapter useful to consider.

There is an old adage, "It's not what you're eating; it's what's eating you."

As that saying goes, you may want to, or need to, figure out why you overeat, especially if in the past you have found it difficult to keep off the weight that you lost once you'd achieved your ideal weight.

For those who feel empty inside for whatever reason, food can become a way to try to fill up. Of course you cannot fill yourself emotionally with food, so a cycle begins: trying to fill up with food leads to overeating, which leads to being overweight, which leads to self-loathing, which leads to more overeating.

You cannot buy love, but you can buy food. You can keep replenishing the kitchen cupboard. Food is something you can control a lot more than the friends and family members in your life, or the business or school challenges which are often unpredictable and may seem to be completely outside your control.

Learning to rely upon oneself and not turning to food to solve one's problems, whether those problems are a feeling of emptiness or being overwhelmed with stress, is a step toward returning food to the place it should have in one's life: a means for nourishment and health, and also a source of pleasure.

I also learned that for me there were childhood experiences that factored into my ambivalence about being attractive. But that wasn't the whole reason I had become obese, nor would unlocking the reasons behind my overeating instantly stop my need to overeat. Overeating had become a bad habit for me and, like all habits, especially the destructive ones, it takes time and concentrated effort to break it, and replace it with new, positive ones.

Food is supposed to be a way of sustaining life because you need to eat to live. But for most of us with weight challenges, food has probably taken on another role in our lives as something we turn to when we are sad, lonely, bored, angry, stressed, happy, anxious, worried or grieving. Turning to food, especially the high-caloric variety, when we are not hungry, is a major cause of being overweight or obese.

The first step is to face the reason or reasons that you eat that are unrelated to hunger. Take the self-quiz that follows to learn more about the reasons behind your emotional eating. (Rank from #1, the most important, to the least important, giving each answer a number ranking. Add in for "other" reasons any reasons you have that are not on the list.)

_____ Boredom
_____ Loneliness
_____ Rage
_____ Anger
_____ Stress
_____ Isolation
_____ Poor habits
_____ Anxiety

_____ Depression
_____ Happiness
_____ Grief
_____ Other (fill in)
_____ Other (fill in)

The everyday *misuse* of food for dealing with loneliness, anxiety, stress, and rage can also pile on the pounds—unless there is purging, as in the case of the eating disorder bulimia, which can lead to grave physical and emotional problems.

When food is used as a sedative, almost like a drug, rather than for its nutritional value, it gets harder and harder to even recognize when real physical hunger is being experienced.

When food and overeating take on another role besides nourishment, not only are the underlying reasons for overeating ignored or concealed, but excess weight or obesity along with compulsive overeating, and even bingeing may be the negative aftermath of such uncontrolled "emotional eating".

If you are using food to deal with stress, boredom, loneliness, rage, anger, depression, rejection, fear, or guilt, you are also failing to deal with the underlying problems that are causing you to overeat as well as creating a secondary, related problem of extra weight.

You may need to seek professional help to understand *why* you turn to food to deal with those feelings.

Mary Anne Cohen, founder of the Brooklyn, New York-based The New York Center for Eating Disorders, and author of *French Toast for Breakfast: Declaring Peace with Emotional Eating*, shares her own background as a child who saw herself as overweight; although looking at pictures of herself now, she realizes she was not that heavy. But as a child and a teenager, she learned to sneak food. *French Toast for Breakfast* is about her journey to learn how to only eat when she was hungry, a journey she has been helping others with for the last thirty years.

Cohen shares in her book these examples of emotional eating:

- Emotional eating is when you are lonely in the middle of the night and you look for comfort in the refrigerator.
- Emotional eating is when you are angry with somebody and you tear and chew into food when what you really want is to bite that person's head off…
- Emotional eating is using food to distract or detour yourself from, or deny your inner problems.

Learning to allow yourself to feel the emotions, rather than turning to food to avoid the feelings, is a very big step. When you stop overeating, and especially emotional eating, feelings may emerge that are scary or unfamiliar to you. That is why you may want to consider participating in a self-help group for those with overeating problems, or working with a trained therapist who has the expertise needed to help you through these powerful feelings.

Emotional eating also has consequences for those who are not overweight. A twenty-six-year-old college student shared with me, even though she is considered thin and has never had an overweight problem, why she would like to stop her pattern of emotional eating:

> I eat when I'm bored or am feeling sorry for myself. It can't be good to turn to food when you hurt emotionally. But I have no physical repercussions from eating ten cookies, so I haven't done anything to change my behavior.

Since she does not solely turn to food when she's upset, she doesn't think of it as a problem. She is aware, however, that if her naturally fast metabolism ever slowed down, weight gain would become an issue; her habit of turning to food when she is not hungry but instead, for emotional reasons, might at that point lead to a weight gain.

Losing weight and keeping it off, particularly if you have to learn to deal with your feelings in non-food ways, can be a painful experience, especially initially. But remember we are playing down the concept of a "diet". Creative weight management means partaking in a medically sound and supervised program of healthy eating and regular exercise suited to your health status, activity level and lifestyle.

What Are You Feelings When You Eat Even If You Are *Not* Hungry?

It may help you on your path to self-discovery about your relationship with food, eating and overeating to see the pattern behind your eating when you are not hungry, and what you are feeling at that time.

Keep track of your food consumption beyond your basic three meals a day for nourishment. If possible, follow yourself for one complete day and evening, since it is easy to leave out key details if you try to create a food diary retroactively.

Write down the specific time, what you are eating or drinking, how you are feeling, and if you are hungry.

Food Diary for (date/day)______________

Time	Place	Food or Beverage	Hungry?

What emotion do you feel?

For what reason are you eating?

__________	__________	__________	__________
__________	__________	__________	__________
__________	__________	__________	__________
__________	__________	__________	__________
__________	__________	__________	__________

_______________ _______________ _______________ _______________

_______________ _______________ _______________ _______________

_______________ _______________ _______________ _______________

_______________ _______________ _______________ _______________

_______________ _______________ _______________ _______________

Do you see a pattern as to when you are eating and why (the times that you answered 'no' to being hungry)? Perhaps you are eating when you are not hungry, as soon as you are getting home after work, out of anger, stress, rage or loneliness?

Perhaps you are eating from 8–10 p.m. when you are sitting in front of the TV out of boredom, loneliness or habit?

Maybe you emotionally eat when you're on the telephone and bored with the conversation, but you do not know how to politely get off the phone? Or maybe you eat when you are stressed and fear you'll say the wrong thing if you don't calm yourself down with food?

Try to see a pattern to your emotional eating so you can begin to understand how, when, and why you are turning to food when you start to feel a certain way, but you dispel those feelings with food. Are you more likely to overeat on weekends? When you eat out? Between the hours of four and seven, when you're waiting for your spouse to arrive home? What other activities might you engage in besides overeating to deal with your feelings of anxiety, stress, loneliness, or boredom?

Perfectionism

In their article, "The Role of Stress in the Association between Low Self-esteem, Perfectionism, and Worry, and Eating Disorders", physicians Sandra Sassaroli and Giovanni Maria Ruggiero point out that two of the key psychological features of people with eating disorders are **perfectionism** and **low self-esteem.**

They note that in the widely quoted 1990 study by

Frost, Marten, Lahart and Rosenblate, six dimensions of the perfectionism that is behind eating disorders include:

1. Personal high standards
2. Concern over mistakes
3. Parental criticism
4. Parental expectations
5. Doubts
6. Organization

Needing everything to be perfect can sabotage a weight loss and maintenance program because often attached to that perfectionism is the "Well, I wasn't perfect today, so I might as well eat everything and anything I want" syndrome. The problem is that what you do in response to your less-than-perfect efforts is often far worse than your original imperfections.

Perfectionists are very hard on themselves. In their article noted above, Sassaroli and Ruggiero, again citing the study on perfectionism by Frost, *et al.*, write: "Pathologic perfectionists allow little room for making mistakes and perceive even minor ones as likely to lead to a future final failure. Thus, pathologic perfectionists never feel that anything is done completely enough or well enough, and their actions are always accompanied by feelings of self-criticism and a sense of ineffectiveness."

Perhaps you are not a "pathologic perfectionist" but instead you are a perfectionist to enough of a degree that it interferes with your weight control efforts as you apply an unrealistically high standard of perfection to your daily eating plan.

Possible Solutions

Instead of perfectionism, strive for excellence. Instead of being so hard on yourself and whether or not you have a perfect body, appreciate yourself. Even after you lose most of the excess weight, there might be imperfect aspects of your body. By accepting your imperfections, you'll be less likely to say, "Why bother, if I can't be perfect anyway?" Yes, you want your brain surgeon to be precise and you also don't want to miss even one typographical error if you're a proofreader, but the difference between those examples of 100% accuracy and the perfectionist is that the perfectionist has unrealistic standards that cannot be met; it is sadly too easy to give up completely if something is not absolutely perfect. Food translation of perfectionism sabotaging weight challenges: you eat too much in one day, so why even try to go back to working the program?

Plan for imperfection. If you are a perfectionist, you may want to plan how you will deal with yourself if and when you do have an occasional slip, or if on a particular day you don't follow your weight loss program *perfectly*. Remember, since no one is perfect, it's bound to happen at some point. It might happen on day 5, on day 55, or on day 155. Having ways to deal with your imperfections in place may help you once your diet is in full swing if you have an imperfect day.

Best advice? Get right back on your weight loss plan and put the imperfect meal, day, or even days, behind you. This means accepting that you're not perfect and going back to following your program rather than punishing yourself for your imperfections by eating more or, worse yet, abandoning your efforts to take off the weight, and keep it off.

Get help for your perfectionism. Perfectionists are often very controlling people who can be as hard on others as they are on themselves. Learning how to accept your own, and others', imperfections will help more than just your weight challenges; it will also help your relationships and your career. Living with, or working for, a perfectionist can be tough on those around her or him. If you are a perfectionist, getting help for it will definitely help others as well.

If you are living with, or working for, a perfectionist, you can also get help. In that way, you can learn some coping mechanisms, so you are not drawn into his or her unrealistic standards that you probably never seem to meet. You can learn how to protect your self-esteem so if you want to continue the personal or work relationship, it will not negatively impact you (and possibly even cause you to eat more).

Low Self-esteem

Therapist Marilyn J. Sorensen, founder of The Self Esteem Institute and author of *Breaking the Chain of Low Self-Esteem*, defines self-esteem as "the view or picture you have of yourself as competent, adequate, deserving, worthy and lovable".

Why is it so important to deal with low self-esteem if you want to lose weight and keep it off?

The first reason is that having higher self-esteem will increase the likelihood that you see yourself as deserving of a trim body with an attention-getting wardrobe. If you do not feel you are worthy of having a nice figure and being the center of attention, you may find it hard to reach your goal or, once you reach it, to maintain your goal without reverting to your old habits and regaining all the weight.

A second reason is that losing weight and dressing in a way that increases the attention that you get will be more pleasant if you have high self-esteem. If you have low self-esteem, you may find getting attention a negative experience, which could decrease the positive outcome of losing weight and staying healthy even if you do maintain your weight loss and not backslide.

Think about yourself. Do you currently have high, medium or low self-esteem? If you currently have low self-esteem, what are the ways that you see this may be impacting on your current weight and your weight management goals?

Have you ever had higher self-esteem?

If yes, when?

What happened to cause you to have lower self-esteem now?

Possible Solutions

Begin by exploring the causes of your low self-esteem. If useful, work with a trained therapist or eating disorder expert on this issue.

Look at the relationships in your life and consider if they raise or lower your self-esteem. Are your family members making you feel good about yourself? If not, can you talk to them about the way they treat you so you will feel better about yourself? If your friends do not appreciate you, and you cannot adjust with the way they treat you, consider finding new friends who will help you have high self-esteem or who won't adversely impact the self-esteem you do have.

Break the cycle of low self-esteem by looking at your parents and seeing if they had low self-esteem that they passed on to you by association. No one is born with low self-esteem. It is a learned attitude. If you learned to have low self-esteem, you can now learn to have high self-esteem (and to pass on that high self-esteem self-perception to your own children and loved ones).

As psychoanalyst and psychotherapist Carolynn Hillman writes in *Recovery of Your Self-Esteem*: "As you were parented, so you parent yourself." If your parents were critical, negative, and neglectful, you probably learned to feel self-loathing and to be overly self-critical. Your low self-esteem is a product of those early years.

Try to confront your low self-esteem and turn it around with a plan, like Hillman's ten-step program. To break the cycle, and to develop high self-esteem, or at least higher, Hillman suggests a ten-step program that includes:

- recognizing your good points and believing in yourself

- looking at how you berate yourself
- recognizing the real you
- finding out who taught you to have negative feelings about yourself
- learning what you require to feel nurtured, and
- developing the skills for empathic communication so you will listen with your emotions and talk so others will really hear you.

(For a complete list of the ten steps, as well as detailed suggestions for carrying out each step, read Part 2, Chapters 4-12 in Hillman's useful book, *Recovery of Your Self-esteem.*)

Exploring Your Psychological Weight Profile

Questions to ask yourself:

Do you know what's eating you—what's causing you to overeat?
If yes, make a list of those possible causes:

____

____

____

What triggers your uncontrolled overeating? Stress? Frustration? Feeling helpless? Anger? Traveling?

Do you have poor eating habits that you need to change? Make a list of those habits:

____

____

____

Is depression causing you to eliminate exercise from your life (even though exercise might actually help you to feel less depressed)?

Are you dealing with the feelings that being thin brings up

so when you get thin you are more likely to stay that way?

Do you feel comfortable when you are complimented on your appearance?

Documenting Your Weight History

While conducting research for this book, here are excerpts from an e-mail I received from Brenda*:

> Up until ten years ago, I never had a weight problem. In high school, I "thought" I was overweight, but for my height and build, I was actually perfect. Wish I had known that back then! I was tall and slender but had the curves in all the right places.
>
> That is what makes this weight gain so devastating for me. I know what it feels like to be thin and healthy, and being the way I am now is just very defeating for me. I got pregnant with my first child ten years ago at the age of 21. Due to some problems, I was put on bed rest for the last half of the pregnancy. I remember at the end of the pregnancy the doctor looked at me and very nastily said, "Do you want to weigh over 200 pounds when this is all done?"
>
> Of course I didn't, but I didn't know what I was supposed to do! I never had to think about what I was eating before; what had changed? He had me eating certain things each day, and I was on total bed rest. Talk about a losing situation. After I had my son, I leveled out at about 180 pounds, so I was about 40 pounds overweight. At that time, I began my years of yo-yo diets… With each pregnancy, I added more weight until I reached my present

*A fictitious name is being used to protect the anonymity of those quoted in this book from my original survey or interviews.

> weight of 245…
>
> Until you deal with a weight problem, you just don't understand how much it affects your life. Not just in the clothing and activity departments, but also just interacting with new people. You wonder if they are looking at you and feeling pity or hatred or just what…because you are overweight. It is very defeating…

I am sharing Brenda's story because I want you to see how unique each story is and yet how similar. What is your weight history? Jot down some of the biggest events and feelings you have related to your weight, right up to today, this moment.

My Weight History

Start with your first memory related to your appearance. How old were you at the time? Do you know what you weighed? Were you considered overweight or within the healthy guidelines for your age, height and frame? Do you remember how you felt about yourself? Overweight? Average weight? Underweight?

____

____

____

____

How old were you when you felt like your weight had become "a problem"? Can you recall any incidents or comments that any friends, schoolmates, family members or strangers made about your weight or your appearance in general? Why did it bother you?

____

____

____

____

____

What about some of the other issues that were going on during your childhood that might have impacted on your weight? Were you popular during your formative younger years? What about during high school? Did you have one or two close or best friends? Were you part of a clique?

When did you start dating? Did you enjoy dating? Did you feel confident about your appearance, or self-conscious?

Did you enjoy buying clothes and dressing in a way that attracted attention?

When's the first time you remember using food to deal with your feelings?

When was the first time you were told that you were fat? Who said it, and why? What did you say in response? How did it make you feel?

How many times have you been on a diet?

How long do you usually stay on a diet?

How much weight do you currently want to lose?

Does anyone else in your family of origin have a weight problem? Your mother? Father? Sibling? If yes, describe the nature of his or her problem in terms of how many pounds overweight or underweight he or she is, how it impacted your childhood, as well as how it influences your relationship today?

Are there any experiences in childhood or adolescence that you avoided because of your weight?

When's the time that you remember being your preferred weight? How old were you? What did it feel like? How long did it last?

Have you ever attended a class or seminar to deal with your weight challenges? If you did, what was it like?

Do your close or best friends have weight problems? If yes, what are their challenges?

When's the last time you went swimming in a swimsuit and felt confident about your appearance?

Use this space to write as much about your weight history

as possible. (If this is a library book, if you prefer to write in your computer than in the book, record your history in another location but try to take the time to tell your story. It will help you to have a starting point in this new weight loss and maintenance journey.)

____

____

____

____

____

____

____

____

____

____

What is your food personality?

Considering what your food personality is might give you some insight into your attitudes towards food. Here are some types to consider:

- **Compulsive overeater:** Do you eat and continue to eat even if you're no longer hungry?
- **Feast or famine dieter:** Are you the kind of eater who either can't get enough of food and continues eating almost until it hurts or the dieter who thinks eating anything at all is "too much" so you think you are dieting by following a healthy plan but you are really starving yourself?
- **"I just pick" eater:** Do you tell everyone that you "just pick", but you're really consuming lots of food when no one's looking?
- **Carboholic (craves carbohydrates):** Do you crave carbohydrates?

- **Sweet tooth:** Do you crave sweets? If yes, what kind?
- **Boredom eater:** Do you eat out of boredom, rather than hunger? If yes, is there a pattern to your boredom eating?
- **Controlled and overly-orderly eater:** Do you need to know exactly what and when you will eat so that parties or vacations cannot throw you off track because so much of the food experience is unplanned?
- **Rage eater:** Do you eat out of anger rather than hunger? Do you eat when you are angry at someone in your current life, whether related to work or your intimate relationships, or is your rage eating based on deep-seated residual anger from your childhood and teen years that were less than ideal?
- **Old habits die hard:** Do you continue to overeat even though you've dealt with the issues behind your overeating? Do you keep up your old, poor eating habits even though you have changed?

Look over your answers. What do you see as your main food personality?

What might cause you to be like that?

What can be done about it to help increase the likelihood of success on a weight loss and management program?

How can you craft new, healthier scripts and food personalities?

A thirty-two-year-old British woman I interviewed who lives and works in London, and who is married, with one child, is an example of someone who has finally conquered her weight issues, which included compulsive eating and overeating. She has maintained her preferred weight for eight years although most of her life she has been overweight, overeating because of anger, isolation, boredom, loneliness, and a craving for sweets. She comments on how she used to misuse food for emotional reasons over the years, which led to the 50 pounds of excess weight that she finally lost and has kept off:

> [I was] always a "tubby" child. Started eating for comfort. Snowballed from there. After leaving university, my weight problem worsened as I was living alone and ate through boredom/loneliness. Also I didn't complete my maintenance [training after a weight loss], so I didn't learn to keep my weight down.

Binge Eating Disorder (BED) and Compulsive Eating (Food Addiction)

Both compulsive eating and binge eating disorder (BED) will sabotage your weight loss and maintenance efforts; they are not exactly the same things, although they are related. Compulsive eating means you eat compulsively even if you're not hungry. You eat for emotional reasons; you eat out of habit. Binge eating disorder means that you suddenly feel an uncontrollable need to eat and you eat an enormous quantity of food in a short period of time.

A 23-year-old accountant I interviewed, who has been overweight her entire life and would like to lose 30 pounds, shared with me about her bingeing:

> I had no control over my eating habits. I would binge. Plus I work a lot, so grabbing chips and chocolate as a snack when working late was real easy.

You may suffer from one or both of these. Either one, unless you get a grip on it, will sabotage your weight loss efforts, either preventing you from staying on your diet or, once you achieve your goal, getting in the way of your lifelong maintenance of your goal weight. The similarity between the two eating disorders is that the eating is out of control.

How do you deal with either or both of these eating disorders?

The first step is to recognize that you even have either of

these problems. The defense mechanism of denial, discussed briefly in Chapter 2, may be at work here in causing you to deny that you are a compulsive eater or a binge eater. But in order to deal with either or both problems, you have to accept that the problem exists.

Consider your eating patterns over the last few years, and then ask yourself these questions:

- Have you ever found yourself eating even though you're not hungry just because the food was "there"?
- Do you find you have to finish everything on your plate even after you are full?
- Do you find yourself suddenly eating huge quantities of food in a short period of time not because you're that hungry, but instead, because of an emotional trigger?
- Do you ever hide food and eat it secretly?
- Do you find yourself obsessed about food, thinking about it all the time, worried you might not have enough to eat?

Overcoming compulsive eating and binge eating disorder may require outside help. This outside help may be provided by:

- a trained professional, such as
- a psychologist,
- psychiatrist,
- psychotherapist, or
- social worker; or
- through a support group, such as Overeaters Anonymous, which is a self-help group based on the model of Alcoholics Anonymous and run by peers; or
- a group facilitated by a trained mental health professional with group participants who share the same problem

In a press release from the National Institute of Mental Health, one researcher, Dr Frederick K. Goodwin, stressed that "the majority of obese people do not have a mental disorder" and the guest scientist, Dr Susan Z. Yanovski, found that people with BED were four times as likely to suffer from depression at some point in their lives as those in the general population.

This is connected to my belief that most people whose overweight condition and overeating are caused by something more than poor eating habits, and those who want to lose weight and permanently keep it off may find it necessary to determine what's been eating them (as well as what they've been eating). Fortunately there are experts trained in helping children, teens, men and women to overcome their eating disorders. See the international associations listed in the Resources section of this book; through their websites, or by calling their headquarters, you will be able to get referrals to individuals or treatment facilities for help with your eating-related issues.

Prior Victimization (Sexual Abuse)

Consider another factor that might be behind compulsive overeating. For several years I researched childhood and adolescent sexual abuse by surveying and interviewing adult survivors. The statistic that is generally accepted is that 25 per cent of adult women have been sexually abused as children. Overeating and being overweight is a common reaction to being a victim of sexual abuse. There are between 33 -50 per cent of overweight American adults. Is there a cause and effect between these two statistics?

No one, myself included, is saying that there is such a direct relationship in all instances, but in some cases it may be true. In another completed survey in my weight study, a 31yearold woman, who has been struggling with obesity since the age of twenty-one and is currently 244 pounds —about 100 pounds overweight—writes: "I was molested by a neighbor at age eight, by a step-uncle at twelve, and raped by an acquaintance at age fourteen."

In a previous extensive survey that I conducted of 26 adult

survivors of childhood/teen sexual abuse, along with selected follow-up interviews, I asked respondents to check off any conditions that they had that they thought might be tied to the sexual abuse that they experienced. Everyone who answered that question checked off "low self-esteem" and sixteen had overeating and weight issues, including at least five who shared that they weighed between 200 and 300 pounds. Four more reported being 10 to 30 pounds overweight.

If someone was sexually abused as a child or adolescent, if a perpetrator picked out a victim and sexually abused him/her, it is not a surprise that the victim would grow up with ambivalence about being attractive and singled out.

Here are some ways that being sexually assaulted as a child or a teen could relate to later weight problems in some instances:

- Being sexually abused means you are out of control of your life and your body.
- Eating may be a way to try to regain control.
- Overeating may be a way of trying to regain power and to avoid the acceptance that proved so painful and psychologically damaging.

From my research, as a 43-year-old single social service worker from the West, who is 5'2" and weighs 206 pounds and who was abused by her brother, a family friend, and a healthcare professional from the age of 13 until 16, put it:

> My perfectionism/controlling/compulsive/workaholic behavior are all driven by not wanting to ever be caught off guard again… And the only thing I've ever been able to trust has been food.

Fortunately, there are trained professionals who can help survivors of childhood or adolescent sexual abuse to deal with the aftermath of the experience, including overeating, poor body image, rage, anger, sexual dysfunction. There may also be free telephone counseling or a weekly support group offered for adult sexual abuse survivors, led by trained group facilitators.

Check with your local rape and sexual abuse crisis center, women's center, YMCA, or community center to see if they provide such a service or are able to make a referral to one.

You might want to read my novel, *The Pretty One* (published by Hannacroix Creek Books, Inc. and available in print, electronic, and audiobook versions), which explores in fiction how success catapults the heroine, psychologist Dr Emily Taylor, on a food binge. As her weight climbs up the scale, Emily realizes she needs to deal with the unresolved sexual molestation from her teen years, one of the key unresolved psychological issues behind her lifelong battle with food.

Post Traumatic Stress Disorder (PTSD)

After the horrific attacks on Americans on 11 September 2001, several symptoms began to emerge even in those who were not at the World Trade Center site, but were impacted by the attacks; namely, sleep problems and, pertinent to this book, turning to food for comfort and overeating.

However, experts do not yet confirm a cause and effect between traumatic experiences and the development of an eating disorder. As physicians Rodriguez, Perez and Garcia note in the beginning of their article in the *International Journal of Eating Disorders*, "Impact of Traumatic Experiences and Violent Acts Upon Response to Treatment of a Sample of Colombian Women With Eating Disorders", "…a specific and direct causal relationship between the history of trauma and/or sexual or physical abuse and the subsequent development of an eating disorder has not been demonstrated."

Even though they suggested the results of their findings be viewed with caution because of possible research design limitations, they still found that in the 160 Columbian women between the ages of twelve and forty-nine who were studied, dropout and relapse rates were much higher in those women who reported experiencing previous traumatic events (sexual or physical abuse, being the victim of a violent crime or having a family member who was a victim).

Getting Help

There are excellent mental health professionals who specialize in the understanding and treatment of eating disorders. I am not trying to compete with those professionals in this chapter. This chapter is not in any way meant to be a substitute for seeking out a trained eating disorder expert or therapist, if you need one. Rather, this is a very general overview of some of the psychological issues that may be behind overeating or weight problems to start you thinking about possibly seeking out an expert to discuss your weight issues.

Remember that the treatment options cover a wide range, from one-on-one individual therapy to being in a group led by a trained professional, or a self-help group. There are also weekend seminars led by researchers and therapists in the weight challenge field as well as seminars or conferences you can attend. There are extensive excellent books that deal with the psychological issues behind overeating and weight problems, such as *Fat and Furious* by Judi Hollis, *Making Peace With Food* by Susan Kano, *Father Hunger: Fathers, Daughters & Food* by Margo Maine, Ph.D., and *A Starving Madness: Tales of Hunger, Hope and Healing in Psychotherapy* by Judith Rabinor, Ph.D., among others. (For additional resources, see the Bibliography at the end of this book.)

4

THE SOCIOLOGY OF WEIGHT ISSUES

There may be individual psychological reasons behind overeating, obesity, or eating disorders, but obesity and eating disorders (bulimia, bingeing, anorexia nervosa) have also become an international problem, with obesity increasing worldwide, although at different rates in each country. Everyone knows that in the United States, except for the state of Oregon, where obesity levels have remained consistent, there has been a steady increase in the number of obese Americans. The current rate of obesity in the United States is put at more than one-third of adults and 17 per cent of youth, according to an article by Cynthia L. Ogden, Ph.D., et. al. in the *Journal of the American Medical Association*.

What are some of the trends in a culture or society that might be a factor in these causes of obesity?

- Inactivity
  How much does a society promote walking or bicycle riding to work or school, and how much reliance is there on driving everywhere—even the shortest distances?
- Poor nutrition
  What food is the norm for that culture? Is the available fast food low-cost, healthy, and low-calorie, or is it only high-calorie and with a high fat content?
- An overemphasis on quick results, which may not be long-lasting when battling weight
  Losing weight and making permanent changes in habits that are more likely to lead to lifelong positive changes

take time. An overemphasis on fast results can make it harder to stick to a slow but effective diet. Not only may it be harder to maintain fast weight losses, but if certain types of foods or behaviors are temporarily put aside for quick results, there may be a rebound effect with a craving for a food that was eliminated or a behavior development where moderation was not learned.

- Eating well (and healthy) usually requires more income for the higher-cost protein foods than eating the lower-cost (but higher in calorie) starches and carbohydrates. In general, it costs more to eat healthy. But it is actually less expensive in the long run since you are minimizing or eliminating health costs that arise from weight-related illnesses or diseases.
- Educating the public about healthy eating and exercise needs to be more of a priority at the local, state, and federal levels of government.
  Learning how to eat healthy and how to cook nutritious foods should be national priorities at every age level and in every socioeconomic group.
- Some employers are putting healthy eating and exercise as a priority concern in their workplace environments, but it needs to be more prevalent.
  Exercising during the lunch hour should be encouraged, as well as making available more on-site exercise facilities, and healthy foods in company cafeterias.
- The earliest group—the family—can impact children's attitudes about themselves in positive or negative ways, which in turn impacts their eating habits.
  Control issues between parents and children are too often centered on food, which can lead to lifelong eating challenges. If parents do not offer a good example of healthy eating, as noted before, children can pick up poor eating habits.

- Better ways of dealing with stress, besides overeating, need to be taught.

  Because food is legal, there is much less concern about helping someone who is turning to food to deal with stress than to other substances, e.g. illegal drugs or over-the-counter pills.

There is an encouraging trend in corporate America to teach meditation and yoga as a way of reducing stress. Aetna C.E.O. Mark Bertolini, as reported by David Gelles in his book, *Mindful Work*, excerpted in *The New York Times* on 1 March 2015, introduced meditation and yoga to his 50,000 employees. More than 13,000 employees have taken one of the free classes. Aetna has reported that participation in those free meditation and yoga classes has reduced stress, health claims, and increased productivity.

- The main focus on weight loss is on the appearance factor. Losing weight and keeping it off needs to be emphasized as a health goal rather than primarily a beauty or fashion issue.
- Watching TV is a predictor of obesity in children, according to a New Zealand study.
  A long-term study of 1,000 children who were born in 1972 found that it was not the sedentary aspect of watching TV that led to the increased likelihood of obesity, but the consumption of food that was associated with watching TV.
- Dieting at too young an age
  A three-year study of nearly 17,000 children in the United States from ages nine to fourteen, reported in *Time* magazine, found that 30 per cent of the girls and 16 per cent of the boys were on a diet. However, when the frequent dieters were compared to children who were not dieting, they were actually more than 2.5 pounds heavier

than their peers. The probable reason for this was that the "overly restrictive diets led to cycles of binge eating".

Food and Socializing/Special Occasions

We have come to associate food with socializing and special occasions—everything from weddings and graduation parties to the extensive spreads we expect after a funeral. That food consumption has social elements to it, although it is important to learn how to deal more effectively in those social situations if you want to reach, and stay at, your preferred weight.

For example, my weight loss and maintenance program facilitator, Mary, shared with our group the story of her cousin, Joey. Joey decided one holiday season not to pay attention to what he was eating at all the family gatherings. So from Thanksgiving through Christmas and New Year's, he ate anything he wanted at all the family gatherings. His weight gain between November and January? Over 22 pounds. Mary assured us that Joey was not going to do that again.

The Prevalence of Being Overweight and Obesity Differs Among Populations

According to the US Department of Health and Human Services, there is a higher tendency towards being overweight, and obesity, among racial/ethnic minorities in the US, particularly minority women, than among whites. Asian Americans have a lower overweight and obesity prevalence compared to the entire population.

An article by Elaine Sciolino, "France Battles a Problem That Grows and Grows: Fat", in the 25 January 2006 *The New York Times*, points out that incidences of being overweight and obesity had grown in France, though not equally in all regions of the country. According to 2003 estimates, the town of Roubaix has an average of 51 per cent of the population who are obese or overweight compared to the national average of 42 per cent. (In the United States, 65 per cent of the population is considered overweight or obese.) An estimated 55,000 French die annually in obesity-related illnesses. According to the article, unless something changes in France, in fifteen years, the French may have the same prevalence of obesity as the Americans.

The Stigma of Being Overweight and Obese

In societies where being thin is seen as fashionable, and those who are overweight or obese are considered less worthy, weight becomes a way that children, teens, and adults are judged, and judge themselves. Just as those who are seen as too thin are stigmatized, being considered overweight or too fat is stigmatizing as well. Recently, I saw an obese woman interviewed on a talk show who shared how she was denied employment because of her 100+ extra pounds. Another talk show guest was suing the airlines because they required that she purchase two seats when she booked a flight.

A few years back, there was talk of the great divide based on whether or not someone had access to a computer at home, especially among children, teens and college students, who needed a computer to keep up with their studies. There are lots of local and national philanthropic programs that are trying hard to get computers into all schools and even refurbished computers into the homes of all students. But what about the social divide among those who have a "normal" figure, compared to those who are 10-to-20 pounds overweight, or who are obese?

Yes, the stigma of being overweight and obese (or underweight) is unfair. Everyone has the right to be treated equally and to be perceived as valuable and treated with respect. The sad situation, however, is that if you are overweight, obese, or too thin, you will probably be stigmatized for it. People may stare at you if you are too thin or too fat. You may feel their looks and find it unpleasant and impolite, but that is what may happen. You may be the subject of nasty comments. When I became severely overweight—yes, I'll use the word, even obese—I had certain individuals ignore me even though I knew we had seen each other in passing. That same person, once I lost the weight, would engage in a conversation with me, taking me in, being chatty and pseudo-friendly.

Remember that it is truly *their* problem, not yours. The stigma hurts, and it is wrong. Yes, you can spend a lot of time and energy fighting for the rights of overweight, obese, or too thin individuals to be treated equally, but please also put your time and energy into getting the preferred weight you want for yourself for health and any other reasons that you want it. Once you get to your preferred weight, promise yourself that you will continue to be kind and caring toward those who are still obese, overweight, or underweight. You were there once. You know what it was like. Promise yourself that you will not stigmatize those who are not "perfect".

5

OVERCOMING BLOCKS TO SUCCESSFUL CREATIVE WEIGHT MANAGEMENT

Do you ever wonder why some people succeed at dieting and keeping the excess weight off, while others fail, regaining the weight again and again? Do you wonder why some can't even begin a diet, or if they do, cannot stick with it, even for a day?

To help you with your focus on doing something about your weight challenge, it might help to gain a better understanding into what got you to this point in the first place. For example, I have observed that many of the same blocks to creative time management can block someone's successful weight management, such as poor planning, denial, impatience and low frustration tolerance, boredom, selflessness and defensiveness.

This chapter presents each block, and offers insights as well as possible solutions, to help you deal with these common obstacles to creative weight management. By dealing with these blocks, you will increase the likelihood that you will be able to successfully diet until you reach your ideal weight, as well as be able to maintain it.

Look over all the blocks listed below that will be covered in this chapter. Then read about those blocks that you think apply to you or, if you think it will be helpful, all of these possible stumbling blocks. Who knows! You or someone you love or care about may have a block that you were unaware of until you saw it described in this chapter. After all, *self-awareness* is one of your best weapons in your fight against being overweight or obese, creeping obesity (whereby the pounds gradually come on until, one day, you're again severely overweight), or the yo-yo dieting syndrome of going down the scale only to go right back up again, and then back down.

This chapter describes the following weight management traps. It will also offer insights into possible causes, as well as some suggestions for solutions, to overcome each one:

- Denial
- Procrastination
- Negative thinking
- Poor planning
- Giving others too much credit or blame for your success (or failure)
- The inability to say "no"
- Impatience and low frustration tolerance
- Fear of failure
- Fear of success
- An inability to take compliments (or criticism)
- The couch potato (sedentary) syndrome
- Bad habits
- Devaluing or overvaluing your accomplishment
- Boredom
- Defensiveness
- Selflessness
- Jealousy
- Perfectionism *(see Chapter 4)*
- Low self-esteem *(see Chapter 4)*

Denial

Have you ever seen a woman or a man weighing upwards of 300 or 400 pounds and wondered how anyone could weigh that much? Didn't they stop and decide to do something about their weight along the way to that dangerously high number? How could someone get to weigh that much? No one wakes up and suddenly weighs a few hundred more than he or she did the night before.

But, along the way, someone gained those extra pounds and became overweight or obese, whether it took days or weeks to gain a few pounds or months or years to gain a whole lot more.

Denial helps us avoid seeing what we weigh, or dealing with our problem.

Denial is a defense mechanism whereby someone denies something is true or even that a problem exists. It is an unconscious way the mind deals with situations or emotions that are just too difficult to comprehend. A child, even if his or her parents are constantly fighting, may deny they have an unhappy marriage because to entertain that thought introduces too much anxiety into his or her life, as he or she needs to believe that parents will always be together and will always have a home with the child. We know that battered spouses, despite their bruises, often deny there are problems because it would require them to make changes in their marriages and lifestyles that are too overwhelming and frightening to consider.

Denial is a powerful defense mechanism.

When it comes to facing what you weigh, or the need to go on a diet, denial sabotages healthy weight management.

Denial allows you to keep your head in the sand.

Possible solutions

Facing reality is the first way you can combat denial, and begin, or continue, the changes that will get you where you want to go. You need to face what you weigh in order to make changes.

It doesn't help to look in the mirror and say, "I can't believe my thighs could get so fat in just a few months."

Reality is, "What am I going to do about these fat thighs?"

Facing reality doesn't mean that you start beating yourself up or having negative thoughts. But it does mean that you avoid denial as a way of putting off taking the necessary positive steps that will improve how you feel, your health, your self-esteem, and how you look.

Getting on the scale may help you avoid denial by keeping you in tune with reality. The scale provides neutral numeric information about your body, but it should not be used for self-downing or excessive negative thinking about just how far you have to go to reach your goal weight. It's important not to deny how much you weigh, so that you can truly start to focus on realizing your goal of diminishing the number that the bathroom scale is stuck at. The bathroom scale does not have to be kept in the bathroom either. Put it in your bedroom or wherever you are more likely to get on it at the same time of day wearing the same clothes, or without clothes, for consistency.

Using a food scale may similarly help to keep you grounded, to avoid denying just how large, or small, a portion you are consuming.

Keeping track of what you are eating by using measuring spoons or cups also makes you aware about just how much you are eating or drinking. Recently, I weighed my dinner portion of protein. I was sure it was at least 4-5 ounces. Instead, it was just two. I was glad I used the scale or I would have blamed myself for being insatiable or put myself down for being ravenous instead of meeting the reality of needing to increase the amount of protein for that meal.

Have someone take your picture to break through denial and keep yourself anchored to reality. It can be shocking to see yourself through the camera's eyes, but it may be necessary to have that kind of splash of cold water on you if it will get you moving.

Looking in a full-length mirror, not just looking at your face, may help to combat operating or thinking in denial of your current weight or size.

Seek professional help if the scale says one thing and you deny what that number indicates about your weight, whether the number is much higher or lower than your preferred weight for your height, frame and activity level. You may need someone to guide you through your weight loss and maintenance efforts if your defense mechanism has been denial and that defense is taken away from you when you are jolted into facing the truth about your weight challenge.

Procrastination

Putting off doing something you have to do, procrastination, applies to the weight challenge as you put off starting a weight management program...for another day. (Or tomorrow, next week, or after x, y or z occurs.)

The result is the same: you remain overweight or obese, or even gain more weight, rather than tackle this goal, which is crucial to your health.

Instead of beating yourself up over being a procrastinator, it is a big step to ask yourself: what benefits do I get from procrastinating? If you put off dieting, you do not have to deal with the disappointment that might occur if you try to diet and fail. Or, for some who have deep-seated fears of being the center of attention and pursued, for reasons that range from shyness to fear of intimacy, putting off coping with the weight challenge also means delaying dealing with those attention issues.

Possible solutions

What are some of the solutions for procrastination that you could apply to your weight challenge?

Figure out what purpose your procrastination is serving. What is it about losing weight and keeping it off that you fear? Are you afraid you'll be hungry while you're dieting? Are you afraid you'll become more attractive than your friends or relatives and they'll be jealous? I remember years ago I taught an evening course in Manhattan and one of my students told me that she had lost 100 pounds, and her husband was very jealous whenever she went out of the house after that. Losing weight brought up all sorts of relationship challenges that she and her husband had put off dealing with all the years she was overweight.

Or perhaps you have tried so many times before to lose weight and keep it off that you are afraid you will fail once again so you are putting off even trying again.

What fear of success issues surrounding your losing weight and keeping it off might be causing your procrastination in starting a weight loss and maintenance program? Are there other goals you've been avoiding dealing with because of your weight issues that you would then have to deal with, like considering whether or not you're in the right career? Have you told yourself, "I'll do this as soon as I lose weight", and if you do lose the weight you would no longer have your weight as an excuse for not doing something?

You will be less likely to procrastinate about beginning your weight management program if you commit to this program as the #1 priority in your life.

If you put doing something about your weight at the top of your "to do" list rather than letting it sit at the bottom as an afterthought that you never get around to accomplishing, you will be less likely to put it off.

Implement the reward system. Reward yourself for even starting a weight management program, the first step you need to take.

Try the buddy system. Ask a relative or a friend to start a weight management program with you so it becomes a joint project. You can cheer each other on and keep each other focused.

Pick a specific target date to start your weight loss and maintenance program so you have something concrete to work with rather than the vague "I'll start tomorrow". If you know you have a particularly stressful week ahead of you, or even a vacation you have to "get through", you might want to pick a start date with as many known stresses behind you as possible. Stress is something we all have to learn to cope with, so you will at some point need to pick, and stick with, a specific date, or this solution for your procrastination about beginning your concerted weight management program will not work for you.

Commit to a specific program, perhaps one that requires you to have formal weigh-ins or appointments, or attend self-help support groups or classes, so you make your weight-related goals specific and definite.

Negative Thinking

Having negative thoughts, or being a defeatist, is probably the number one reason you fail to start a new diet or weight management program, or believe you could ever look, or feel, the way you would like to look. Negative thinking is the opposite of the mindset of the little train in the children's classic tale, *The Little Engine That Could*, which says, "I think I can! I think I can!" as it pulls up that steep, challenging hill.

Positive thinking will take you much further! Being positive and self-assured comes from within. It requires a belief in yourself that is instilled from a very early age by parents and other authority figures and, subsequently, peers who make you feel valuable and competent. Unfortunately, too many start life off surrounded by parents or others, such as siblings, teachers, authority figures, friends, who are negative or defeatist. Then negative thinking becomes almost "inherited" from generation to generation, passed along as surely as parents pass along physical traits.

It's tougher to become a positive person and a positive thinker if you were raised in that kind of a negative atmosphere. You all know the kind of atmosphere I mean. Nothing you did was ever good enough. Instead of saying in a somewhat objective, nonjudgmental way, "How was your day?" there would be a negative innuendo, "Did everything go okay today?" or "Can't you do anything right?"

Negative thinking can have a deep-rooted origin, going back to your earliest experiences where your mother, father, both parents, and even a revered teacher told you that you could not do anything right. You grew up having poor self-esteem and this unfortunately impacts everything you try to do, including losing weight and staying healthy.

You may need more than just a self-help book or even a regulated diet to lose weight and keep it off. You may need to work with a professional therapist who can help you unlock the causes of your negative thinking so you have the positive frame of mind to start, continue, and succeed at a weight loss and maintenance program.

Successful weight management requires a positive attitude. Even getting yourself to Day One requires self-confidence that you can take control over what you eat as well as whether or not you will put more steps into your days by being more active and less sedentary.

Possible solutions

Substitute positive imaging and thinking for negative thinking. Positive imaging goes along with positive thinking. You need to envision yourself as successfully managing your weight, looking fit, and feeling good about how you look and feel.

In order to get to Day One, and stick with it, you need to have positive thoughts.

In case you ever go off your diet, whether you go off for one meal a day, throughout your five-day vacation, or even longer, you need positive thoughts to get yourself back on track.

You need to tell yourself and truly believe that you can, you can, and you can!

Write down five positive things about yourself. If you're having trouble dispelling your negative thoughts, taking a few moments to write down at least five things about yourself that are positive may be helpful. It doesn't matter if it's the way you remember everyone's birthday, the way you put the top back on the toothpaste cover, the enthusiastic way you answer the phone at work, or the way you listened to your friend when she was upset even though you were busy and stressed. Start training yourself to see yourself in a positive light.

Positive things I like about myself:

1. ______________________________.
2. ______________________________.
3. ______________________________.
4. ______________________________.
5. ______________________________.

Turn around negative thoughts. If you start having a negative thought about your weight efforts, catch yourself and transform that thought into a positive one. Write down these thoughts and how you have changed each thought into a positive one.

You could even start catching yourself when you think, speak or write negative thoughts. Turn them into positive statements! It's good training. I had started to write, "Don't let negative thinking sabotage your diet and weight management." Instead, here's the positive version: "Let positive thinking encourage your successful diet and weight management efforts."

Negative thought:

____

____

Rewrite it here in a positive version:

____

____

Work on the roots of your negative thinking. Maybe you can't undo or redo your childhood years and the underlying causes of your negative thinking, but you can look at those causes and decide to have a different way of thinking today. You are not a child anymore. You *can* change yourself. You have the ability to become a positive thinker and doer. Negativity pulls you and everyone around you down. Being positive is better for you and everyone else and it's free! I'm sure you've heard people say, "She's so bubbly. I wish I could bottle her enthusiasm and her positive ways and sell it." Becoming positive is contagious! If you're more positive, you'll find others around you more positive as well.

Poor Planning

This is probably the number one way to sabotage a weight management program. Whether you have 5 pounds to lose, 20, or 100, or more—or if you're at your ideal weight—planning for meals and snacks is essential for your success.

Just as success at work requires that you have a plan—for each day, and for each longer and more complex task you have to achieve, whether it is writing a report, designing a new product, selling a line of wares, or giving the keynote speech at your organization's luncheon—good planning helps to ensure success.

Planning will help you to avoid sabotaging your weight loss and maintenance efforts by being prepared to deal with emotions and situations as those challenges arise. For example, you have to determine what you will do when you get the munchies if grabbing junk food has been one of the downfalls to your weight management program. Perhaps you have to have alternatives to junk food around, such as cut-up vegetables or low-calorie gelatin. Perhaps you need a plan as to what non-food activity you're going to do if you get an attack of the munchies. Take a walk? Call a friend? Read a book? Get on your stationary bicycle machine?

Just as you need to have a budget or plan for holiday spending, you need a plan for how you will spend your daily calories and deal with those situations that often hinder or sabotage your weight management efforts.

Possible solutions

Prioritize planning. The key is to plan and not leave anything to chance and to consider planning an instrumental part of your weight loss and maintenance challenge. Even if you have some "wiggle room" for spontaneity, the best speeches are usually those based on preparation and planning. Similarly, plan what you will eat each day and evening.

Have a plan for parties. If you are going to a big party, plan what you will do if there are only foods you prefer to avoid. Will you bring a fruit or vegetable crudités platter along? Will you eat before you get there so you are not as tempted to eat at the networking (not a dinner) party? Plan what you'll do if you go to a party and you're trying to stay on your program. Will you save up your calories or servings to be able to eat at the party?

Create daily and weekly menus. Map out what you'll eat for each day of the week. Plan what you'll eat as well as what anyone else you have to provide meals for, such as a spouse, children, or elderly parents in your care.

Think about snacks. Think beforehand what you will eat for snacks each and every day.

Create a shopping list so you will buy for your meal plans. Make sure you have the condiments and seasonings you need for cooking as well as the ingredients for the meals you are planning.

Make restaurant choices based on a plan. If you have a choice as to the restaurant you will go to, see if you can find out in advance if you will be able to make choices that facilitate staying on your weight loss program easily. Some restaurants have their menus online, or you could call in advance and ask about how the food is prepared or check with others who have eaten there. Even take-out food can be prepared with your food needs in mind. For example, some Chinese restaurants will create a steamed version of some of their dishes with sauce on the side so you can control how much sauce, if any, you want to add to the dish.

Giving Others Too Much Credit or Blame for Your Success (or Failure)

This obstacle to weight management success is a tricky one because we've all been taught to acknowledge others and show humility—that our success depends perhaps in large part on the efforts of others. But the problem with truly believing that you need others to succeed, or that your success results from having their efforts behind yours, is that it is too easy to blame them when you fail, or give *them* the credit when you triumph. If what they gave you is taken away from you, you may believe you can't do it on your own!

But you can! Whatever anyone has given you, whether it's a diet to follow, a weekly support group to participate in, or a diet journal to record your daily thoughts, the tools to your weight management success only work because *you* apply them. **You have your success in your own hands.** There is no one else who has the answer for you or who will offer you a magical solution. *You* can do it. Yes, you can!

Who will stop you from losing weight and keeping it off?

There's only one person who can stop you from succeeding. It's not your mother. It's not your boss. It's not your children or spouse. It's not even that puppy you adopted that your children promised to walk and care for but you find you're the one doing most of the work!

No, the only one who can stop your weight loss and maintenance plan from succeeding is you!

Possible solutions

Take credit where credit is due. You are also responsible for your success! Not the weight management program you follow. Not the support group you connect to, or the leader you feel cares about your progress. You do need a healthy plan, as we discussed in the last chapter. But that plan is only a guideline. You are the one who has to follow it. If you do follow it, it is your success. It is you who have succeeded, not the plan.

That's important to realize because only if you feel empowered will you succeed, and continue your success, even if, for whatever personal, financial, or other reason, you have to stop, or switch, programs or plans.

I recently reread a questionnaire on weight challenges I had distributed that was completed by a 55-year-old Brooklyn writer. He shared with me that he had lost ten pounds by following one of the famous "high concept" diets named after the place where the doctor had his medical practice. When I asked him how long he kept the weight off, he wrote, "A few days". When I asked him why he put the weight back on, he wrote, "Mainly, I went back to eating too much, and foods that were fattening. Also, I put back on the water weight I had lost."

Bravo that he attributed his relapse to himself and not to the diet! Too often dieters unfairly blame this or that program for failing. It's pivotal to credit yourself for failing *and* for succeeding. In doing so, you are emphasizing that you are the one who is responsible for your weight management. Others may help, or hinder, your goals and progress, but what you put in your mouth, and how much exercising you do, is ultimately a very personal decision and experience.

You are in control!

That's different from saying, "You need self-control". Self-control. We've all heard that word again and again. But saying "You're in control", that has another meaning. It means you're in the driver's seat. *You* control what you eat, when you eat it, with whom you eat, and *why* you eat it.

Avoid getting overly dependent on any one person or program for your success. If you feel it is through your own efforts that you are succeeding, you are more likely to be able to maintain your achievements even if you decide to stop going to a program, or if the leader who cheers you on switches careers and is unable to support you.

The Inability to Say 'No'

There are many dynamics to the "inability to say no*" obstacle to managing your weight successfully. There's the inability to say* no *when someone asks you to try out a rich, fattening dessert that you know will set you back a day or two. There's the inability to say* no *when your family asks if you want to go out for pizza and you know you find it harder to stay in control at a restaurant and you also just had your dinner!*

What can you do?

Possible solutions

Be direct in your *no*. If you're at someone's house and she or he offers you something you don't want to eat, simply say, "No, thank you". You can add "I'm dieting" if you wish, or you can leave out that information.

Learn to say *no* to food. But there's also the inability to say *no* to food. That's what got most of us in trouble in the first place. That food, especially fattening desserts and "emotional" foods, call out to many of us. We look to food for love or as an escape from boredom. We look toward food to make up for what may be lacking in other areas of our lives. Even if we no longer turn to food for emotional reasons, we may have developed the habit of overeating and we are now unable to say *no* to overeating.

If overeating certain kinds of high-calorie foods didn't make us fat (with all the health and social consequences that imply), it probably wouldn't be such a problem. Other than the financial costs of eating too much, it would probably be okay to eat a lot. But overeating does make us fat. Overeating does make us feel as though the food, and not us, is in control.

So it's necessary to say *no* to too much food and the wrong kind of food.

It's helpful to realize that no one likes to say or hear "*No*", but that's what it takes. *No* is not in and by itself a bad thing or a negative thing. It's simply *no.*

Be objective about *no* instead of associating it with a lot of complex emotions. We put all these emotional responses, like rejection, worthlessness, emptiness, and frustration, onto *no*. *No* is simply a way of expressing that you do not want to do something. Try to rid yourself of all the other associations to it.

Impatience and Low Frustration Tolerance

Impatience and low frustration tolerance are obstacles to weight management because they create unrealistic expectations about how long it's going to take to lose the excess weight in the first place, as well as how hard it is to keep it off.

Low frustration tolerance sabotages dieting, and even getting through the first day of your new creative weight management program, Day One, because you turn to food to deal with frustration.

Possible solutions

It may help to look at some of the myths and realities about weight loss and maintenance.

Myth: "I can lose 20 pounds in two weeks."

Reality: A healthy weight loss is 1–2 pounds a week (which translates into 4–6 pounds in a month, tops). (Source: American Heart Association, "Managing Your Weight" booklet, p. 3, "Losing one to two pounds per week is a good rate of loss.") Although you can't safely lose 20 pounds in just two weeks when you follow a healthy diet, you may be able to lose 20 pounds in ten weeks (if you lose only two pounds a week).

Myth: "I can't wait until I reach my goal!"

Reality: Once you reach your goal, you're going to have to work very hard to keep from regaining weight again. You can't suddenly start eating anything you want, or return to old, counter-productive eating habits, if you want to maintain your lower, healthier weight.

Develop the ability to handle more and more frustration, on your own or by working with a therapist. You may have a lower frustration tolerance than others to begin with. That is something that is very tough to change, but it is possible to retrain yourself to handle frustration better. In the meantime, you can find ways to deal with frustration other than food or overeating while trying to increase how much frustration you can tolerate as well.

Fear of Failure

You may be afraid you won't be able to make this diet work—or that you'll lose the weight only to regain it again—so you're reluctant to even try. Be positive! Plan for success. Do whatever it takes to be successful. Don't let your fear of failure freeze you so you are unable to do anything. When it comes to weight, doing nothing, unfortunately, often translates into gaining weight. Very few people are able to eat as much of anything they want without finding themselves gaining weight.

Fear of failure keeps you where you are now, in a place, and at a weight, you no longer want to be. I understand that change can be frightening and unknown. What you have, and are, even if you consciously wish to change it, is safe; most of us give up our safety only with much trepidation.

This fear is tied to the negative thinking that was addressed at the beginning of this chapter.

It is important to rise above all the one or more times you have tried to lose weight and keep it off and failed. Be an optimist! Do things differently this time so you have a chance at a different, and better, outcome.

If you get involved in starting afresh and in the planning related to this diet plan, you may find you can work through your fear of failure. Through your determined efforts, it's more likely than ever that you will succeed this time at reaching your ideal weight and staying there.

Possible solutions

Build up your self-esteem. One cure for a fear of failure is building up your self-esteem so you have the courage to try again. You can do this by constantly looking out for positive things about yourself; congratulate yourself whenever you do something well, or even just for trying. "That cupcake looks delicious, but I think I'll eat a banana instead. Kudos to me for sticking to my diet!" or "I did a really good job dealing with that customer today. She was rude and demanding, but I was calm and polite and settled things the way my manager would. Even though nobody else noticed, it's good to know I can take control of the situation when necessary." By affirming yourself with positive statements instead of looking for validation from others, you are more confident of your abilities and more in control of what you do.

Increase the likelihood you will not fail by putting the time and effort into learning what you have to do and planning for your success. Do everything and anything that you can do to make sure it is more likely that this time you *will* succeed. That means you seek out and follow a medically sound and supervised diet and that you put the time, planning and effort into your diet program, so success is more likely.

Use your fear of failure as a motivator. Rather than immobilizing or paralyzing you, use your fear of failure as a healthy motivator as you strive towards excellence and success.

Fear of Success

Overcoming the obstacle of fear of success requires a lot of mental work. Begin by determining what it is about success that you fear. Don't be surprised if few believe you when you tell them you fear success. "What's to fear?" they may say or think. Think about the times in your life when you were the weight that you long to be now. What about that time? Was it positive or negative? If you understand what those negatives were, it might help you to understand what's behind your fear of becoming that weight again. What associations do you have with achieving your weight goal?

A fear of success is a lot more complex than a fear of failure. Everyone can understand why you would fear failing. Everyone is able to relate to that awful feeling in the pit of his or her stomach associated with failure if they've ever gotten a bad grade at school, misspelled a word and been embarrassed because of it, gotten someone's name wrong or given someone a gift that he or she absolutely hated. The list of potential mistakes is endless.

But what about this fear of success that blocks effective weight management? How do you explain a fear of success? Aren't we all supposed to want success? Aren't you supposed to want to be a smaller size?

Think about success and some of the images that immediately come to your mind. Do you see yourself being more popular? Having others jealous of you? Having to deal with romantic advances? What about coping with the feelings that overeating conceals, but losing weight might bring up?

Possible solutions

Examine what it is about success that you may fear when it comes to losing weight and having the figure that you want. What about all the things you've been putting off because of your weight? If you have been putting off looking for a new job, speaking before a large group, or even making new friends, if you do lose the weight you would no longer have the weight as an excuse. So you may have complicated your weight situation by putting far too many "what ifs" on to your weight problem.

Write down what you fantasize will happen if you do lose weight. By looking squarely and clearly at the success you might fear, and how your weight figures into those fears, you will at least have a better chance at losing weight, and keeping it off, despite those fears.

When I lose weight I will ______________________________

____

When I lose weight I will also __________________________

____

Imagine yourself succeeding despite any of the fears that you associate with success. Empower yourself that you will not let any fears stop you from succeeding, including your fear of success.

An Inability to Take Compliments (or Criticism)

This is an obstacle to successful weight loss and maintenance because an inability to take compliments or criticism may unwittingly stop you from changing. That is because you need to avoid the positive, or negative, comments you may hear along the way down the scale: "You're looking good!", "You've been losing weight, haven't you?", "You're getting too thin". Accept that you will hear comments about your weight loss, and see yourself coping with those comments.

Possible solutions

Put the compliments and criticisms back on the one who is making the comment. Remember, the comment, whether negative or positive, often says more about the person who is making the comment than it does about you.

Examine in detail your reactions to criticism or praise and what may have caused it. Ask yourself: What about a compliment that makes you uncomfortable? What about being noticed makes you squirm? Why is criticism so devastating to you? What was it like for you as a child? Did you grow up in an atmosphere filled with compliments or criticism? If you grew up being criticized, you might actually feel more comfortable when you're being criticized. Compliments may actually be foreign, and uncomfortable, to you. As much as you might consciously want to be thinner, your subconscious pulls may be toward getting criticism for being overweight or obese.

The Couch Potato (Sedentary) Syndrome

We all know that exercise helps the weight loss process as well as keeping the weight off once you've achieved your goal. Being a couch potato and, consequently, failing to exercise has a lot of negative aspects to it. It is an obstacle to creative weight management for numerous reasons, including the fact that eating junk food all too often goes along with excessive television or movie viewing, as well as sitting in front of the computer for too many hours.

Furthermore, since we know that exercising helps to decrease depression—and depression often causes overeating—failing to exercise creates a vicious cycle. The sedentary lifestyle reflected by excessive television, movie, or computer screen viewing goes against the ingredients of a successful and effective weight management program.

A study of 137,593 youths aged 10-16 years old in 34 industrialized countries by Ian Janssen, Ph.D. of Queen's University in Kingston, Ontario, Canada found that the time spent watching TV had a higher probability of being overweight in 65 per cent of the countries. In this study, reported on by Kevin Foley, physical inactivity, rather than eating candy and chocolate, was also a risk factor among youths for an increased likelihood of being overweight.

Possible solutions

Avoid watching TV alone. If you want to watch television, try to do it with others.

Work out while you watch. Position your TV so you can work out at home while you watch. Best of all, try to have a bicycle machine or walking machine within view of the TV set. Work out while you watch, whether you're at home or at the health club with a TV in view. This may even become so habitual that you will soon feel that exercising and watching TV go hand-in-hand.

Place limits on your TV viewing. Try to set limits on how often and how long you'll watch.

Be careful about having food readily available while you watch. Try to avoid having any food, especially fattening junk food, around when you watch. At least go into another room to get a snack, if you get hungry. Make sure healthy snacks are available at all times so you have a chance to make choices that are in the best interest of your priority weight program.

Monitor the time spent at the computer as well as in watching TV. Keep close watch of time spent on the computer, taking breaks every twenty minutes or so, to talk or to moderately exercise.

Bad Habits

For some, overeating is simply a matter of bad habits that have become entrenched over years, even decades.

What are some of the things you do that have caused you to gain weight? Do you snack on high-calorie foods while you watch TV? Do you consume high-calorie drinks? Are you a late-night snacker? Do you fail to keep track of just how much you are eating at each meal, or even what you are eating? When was the last time you had a piece of fruit for dessert or a snack rather than a high-caloric dessert? If you take away all sweets or carbohydrates when you diet, so that you have a "bounce back" situation when you reach your goal of eating anything and everything in sight, are you going to include, in moderation, some sweets or carbohydrates as part of your weight loss program *this time*?

Possible solutions

How do you change bad habits?

The first step is recognizing that you have bad habits. You need to take your habits out of the area of either denial or oblivion. Keep track of how often you grab food without being aware that you're piling on the calories.

The second step is to find out what caused your bad habits in the first place, so you won't revert to them once you reach your weight goal. Find out on your own through introspection or working with a trained therapist or eating disorder expert, the causes of your bad habits.

The third step is substituting new, better habits. That is the benefit of following a medically sound weight program that has ongoing monitoring of your progress. You will have more confidence that the habits you are learning are safe and healthy ones because those plans are based on scientific research. You are being observed so you have someone to report to as you reinforce your new healthier habits. (For a lengthier discussion of changing bad habits, see Chapter 6, "Day One and How People Change", for a discussion of change, which relates to overcoming bad habits as an obstacle to your weight management success.)

The fourth step is sticking with those changes long enough that the new, better habits become routine. Some point to the "21-day" timeframe—"they say" that it takes 21 days, or three weeks, to create a new habit —as the minimum number of days that it takes to replace a new habit for an old one. And there is some scientific basis for this 21-day concept: physician Maxwell Maltz, in his famous book *Psychocybernetics,* theorized, based on observations of his medical patients, that it took patients who lost a limb 21 days to lose a ghost image of the missing limb.

Devaluing (or Overvaluing) Your Accomplishment

Whether you have two, five, ten, 20, 50, 100, or more pounds to lose, taking off excess weight is important, but it isn't the beginning or end of your existence. It's one of the accomplishments in your life. It's one of the challenges you face. For most of us, however, when you lose weight and keep it off, your life will not totally change. You probably won't change careers or communities, although you may change your wardrobe or how you wear your hair.

Losing weight might help your career, especially if you are in a profession or business that frowns on being overweight or obese, but you will still be the same person inside. Putting *too much* value on losing weight, or, conversely, diminishing your accomplishment so you think "Why bother?" are both sabotages to your weight management efforts.

You may increase the likelihood of your weight loss and maintenance success by putting your weight challenges in the proper perspective. Of course you want to give your weight problems the attention this challenge requires and deserves. With any complex and demanding goal, as you are losing weight and doing all the things you have to do to achieve your weight loss, it will especially seem like the most important thing in the world to you. Feeling that way may help you to stay motivated, buying all the necessary foods you need, carefully watching exactly what you put in your mouth, and exercising. But if you *only* value those activities because you're losing weight, you may stop putting in those key efforts once you reach your goal.

Possible solutions

Have a realistic perspective on the value of your weight loss and maintenance efforts. You need to value—not over-value or under-value—all those efforts even once you lose your weight. You will have to continue doing all those same things if you want to manage and maintain your weight for the rest of your life.

Weight management takes effort and achieving the figure you want is a valuable accomplishment that needs to have the value placed on it that is appropriate.

Keep your weight program to yourself until you are ready to share about it. If you have conflicts over placing too much value, or not enough, on your weight loss and maintenance efforts, consider keeping your efforts to yourself until you are comfortable with the comments or pressure that others may put on you.

Boredom

Just as boredom may cause you to waste time, or to stop giving your all to a task or relationship, allowing your weight management program to become boring can have the same impact. Boredom can stop you from starting or staying on a creative weight management program that will give you the short, and long-term, positive changes that you desire.

In this book, you will learn some tricks and techniques for minimizing boredom in your weight management program in Chapter 9, "Moving Toward your Goal". For now, just be on your guard against boredom and plan other activities to do, since it is usually when you are bored that you are more likely to grab junk food to break up monotony, offering a quick fix, but a counterproductive one, to your meal-planning challenges.

Possible solutions

Vary what you eat. To avoid the trap of boredom as a sabotage to your weight control efforts, work at becoming an expert at cooking, or find ways to get delicious, nutritious food that others cook for you, such as take-out, having a family member who likes to cook preparing the meals, or even taking advantage of delicious prepared foods from the supermarket, canned, or in the frozen food departments, that offer variety and excellent nutrition. Try different cuisines. There are literally dozens of options available to you that may fit into your supervised, medically sound food plan.

Vary when and how you take your meals. If you eat at home all the time, try going out more often. If you are always eating out, try cooking for a change. If you like to use prepared frozen or canned foods, try adding other no- or low-calorie ingredients to the foods, so it is not as predictable. If you always eat in the kitchen, try the dining room. If you have a family room that is usually just for watching TV, try serving breakfast, lunch, or dinner there.

Put more effort into the way the food is presented. Create place cards for your meals, even if for just the family. Buy a new tablecloth or placemats to spruce up the table. Flowers can also help make a table less boring.

Try different brands of the same foods. If you like certain types of foods, you could try unique brands of those foods which might taste different even if the calorie counts are the same. For example, there are so many different types of chocolate you can buy. Ditto for ice cream cones, vegetables, fruits, and sources of protein.

Spice your food for variety. Cut down on boredom with varied spices.

Selflessness

Playing the martyr is a block to successful creative weight management by giving you an excuse to ignore your weight problem or putting the time and energy into changing the habits that will enable you to lose weight, and keep it off. You put your focus on others and deny your own needs.

Selflessness, if you use it as an excuse to ignore your weight problem, sends out a negative message to your children, spouse, boss, or co-workers that you are not as valuable as them.

Possible solutions

You need to love yourself in order to love others. It may be a cliché, but it is a true: to love others you need to love yourself first. If you want to teach your children or spouse to respect themselves and each other, or you, you need to show that you love yourself.

Focus on yourself. It is actually more selfless to do what it takes to get healthier, since a healthy weight is tied to increased longevity. Loving yourself begins with eating properly, and making the time to exercise. Your family wants you around. Controlling your weight is one of the habits tied to increasing longevity in a study by Berkman and Breslow of 7,000 residents of Alameda country in California. The other habits included seven to eight hours of sleep, eating breakfast every day, seldom if ever eating snacks, exercising, limiting alcohol consumption, and never smoking cigarettes.

See a little bit of selfishness—putting yourself first—as positive. Rather than being selfish by caring about yourself, you are making sure you will be in better shape, which will enable you to help your family and others more.

Defensiveness

If you are prone to defensiveness, instead of coping with your weight problem, you may spend your time and energy defending yourself, and your right to be overweight, or even the rights of obese people in general. Of course obese or overweight men and women should not be discriminated against, but there are real health, social, and career hazards that this condition poses. Your time and energy will be better spent dealing with your weight problem than defending yourself if someone says something to you about it. Unfortunately, defensiveness may actually cause you to dig in your heels and stubbornly refuse to do something about your weight.

Possible solutions

Give a quick response and move on. Next time you are inclined to defend yourself, if someone says something about your weight, simply acknowledge their opinion, saying something like, "Thank you for your comments. I'll consider what you've said."

Accept who you are and what you are as simply your current reality, whatever your shape or weight. "Own" your current physical condition, so when you are slimmer, you can own that condition as well.

Jealousy

"Such a complicated issue"" begins 30-year-old Beverly in answering "yes" to the question in my survey, "Has your weight ever been an issue in your friendships?" She continues, "Losing weight is about the only goal most of my friends are NOT happy that I've accomplished."

Beverly, who is 5'1" tall, and weighed 126 pounds but wanted to lose 9 pounds, relates what happened when, over the course of a year of working out without even following a specific diet, she was able to achieve the weight of 115 pounds and lose 15.2 per cent body fat:

> Of course my friends noticed my weight changes and felt free to comment on them. At first I was told how great I looked, and gradually they started to turn into comments about how I was "too thin". I really think some of my friends resented my ability to maintain a healthy weight and stay dedicated to my goal… And that's basically what happened constantly: Among several of my girlfriends, if

> you abstain from overeating, you're made to feel guilty. There's a pressure to overindulge. [In] some friends, it is a much more pronounced issue than with others.

We all know that you cannot stop others from being jealous of you, but you could work on coping with those jealous feelings so you do not let someone else's problem sabotage your weight loss and maintenance goals. If a friend, family member, romantic partner, or even a total stranger says or does something out of jealousy, remember: it is *their* problem. Don't make it your problem.

It may also be useful to think back to when you were not working on your weight challenges. Think about it: Were you jealous when someone else achieved the weight loss, or already had the perfect figure, that you so desperately wanted for yourself? It's okay if you admit that you were jealous—and it's okay if you never had those feelings. But if you have ever felt jealous of someone else's figure or weight loss success, you can hopefully be more understanding that the jealousy others may be expressing toward you—with words or even non-verbally, through body language and gestures—is usually not meant in a malicious way. It is simply human nature to want for oneself what others have achieved for themselves.

The one kind of jealous feeling you can directly control, however, are the jealous feelings you have that may be stopping *you* from doing something about your weight. Fantasizing that others can "eat whatever they want" or that they have a personal chef to prepare their meals so losing weight is not that hard for them are just excuses to keep you in the same, unhappy place.

You may find others are jealous of you as you lose weight. What is most confusing is that it may be the very ones who commented initially that you needed to lose weight who are jealous when you achieve your weight goals, making you feel that they liked you better heavier.

Possible solutions

Don't take on yourself the jealousy problems of others. Remember that being jealous of your weight loss success is *their* problem. You can lose weight, and please yourself, or stay overweight or obese, and make others, who have problems dealing with their own jealous feelings, feel comfortable.

Focus on how hard you are working to achieve your goal and you are more likely to feel their jealousy is not warranted. This is not like winning the lottery because you were lucky enough to pick the right numbers. Your weight loss success is based on hard work and concerted efforts—not luck.

Imagine yourself not letting the jealousy derail you. See your acquaintances, friends, family members, business associates, other loved ones, or anyone else that you think may be jealous of your new figure, and imagine yourself dealing with it. That's also a technique to get over fear of success or fear of failure: you imagine the success or failure and see yourself being victorious. Try the same thing with coping with jealousy: see it happening but see yourself dealing with it, without guilt, anger or embarrassment.

Be comfortable with your achievements. Right now, however, take a moment to pat yourself on the back. You've come a long way just since page one! You're putting time and effort into figuring out what blocks you may be experiencing that are stopping you from starting a creative weight management program. Good for you!

Perfectionism and low self-esteem are such prevalent and key causes of weight issues that those conditions are discussed in the next chapter. By exploring what might be behind your weight challenges, you are working up to Chapter 5, "Getting Started" which includes fifteen ways to motivate yourself to begin a healthy weight and exercise program.

6

GETTING STARTED

Creative Weight Management Principle #2:

Prioritize doing something about your weight and eating habits as your #1 concern.

Okay, I'm sympathetic. You have tried so many times before to lose weight, and keep it off, that you have lost track of all those diets. You have spent so much money on weight loss diets or programs, you could have bought two new wardrobes or paid for an amazing vacation staying at five-star hotels in a faraway land with that money by now.

Don't despair! Don't give up! Try again! "What?" you exclaim. "Try *again*?" You can't even get yourself to the point of wanting to try again—let alone actually doing it. You feel defeated. Fed up. Completely negative about the likelihood that you'll *ever* get your weight under control.

Psyche yourself up to try again!

Motivate yourself to give this new creative weight management approach a chance.

Start off by listing why, this time, when you work on managing your weight, that by focusing on healthier eating habits and an improved lifestyle, not just your weight, it may work, even if it worked only once or never worked before. Perhaps you will succeed this time because:

- You're older and wiser.
- You've learned more about weight management.

- You've learned more about yourself.
- You're going to plan more this time.
- You're more aware that this is a very tough challenge.
- You're going to do it this time with a friend.
- You're going to do it this time without a friend (if doing it with a friend sabotaged you last time).
- You're doing it for yourself, not for a special occasion.
- You're more positive about weight management and life in general.
- You're committing yourself to a different medically approved and supervised weight management program this time.
- You know if you don't do something about your weight, it may keep going up, and you don't want that to happen.
- You're practising positive imaging and you're seeing yourself slimmer and willing to do what it takes to make that image a reality.
- You're committed to taking more control over what you eat and when you eat it.
- You're willing to put the time and effort into shopping and cooking for a healthier lifestyle.
- Other reasons not listed above?____________________
  ____
  ____

I hope you've at least convinced yourself to consider giving creative weight management a try. Reread the seven principles that are listed and described in Chapter 3. Make a commitment to yourself and to achieving the new eating and exercise habits that will help ensure you have a lifetime of—not just temporary—fitness.

The next step is motivating yourself to commit to following a *specific* weight management program. We all know that to lose weight you have to eat fewer calories, so your body burns up its reserves of fat for fuel, and exercise more, but we all need expert guidance to follow, like a doctor's written guidance about how many calories to eat, and what food groups, or how many portions of this or that type of food, if it's measured in units instead of calories. We need an expert to tell us *how* to reduce daily calories *without* compromising our health, how much to exercise, and what kinds of activities are safe and in what amounts.

What diet and weight maintenance management plan should you commit to, should you begin? *Any medically sound, supervised weight-loss program will probably work, as long as you stay on it.* But what program will suit *you* best?

Creative Weight Management Principle #3:

Get a medical check-up and pick a medically sound, supervised plan to follow.

Finding the Program for You

As long as it is a well-regarded, medically approved and supervised eating plan, tailored to you and to your medical conditions and, as much as possible, to your food preferences and lifestyle, there are many options available:

- A program suggested and supervised by your family physician or OB/GYN (gynecologist).
- Becoming a member (or client) at any of the medically sound weight reduction programs available throughout the country and the world (see the resource section for a list of programs).
- Working with a nutritionist, dietician, or eating disorder specialist.
- Going to an outpatient or in-patient treatment facility.
- Other options not listed above:____________________
____
____

Find a weight-management program that is best for you the way you would find any healthcare service provider, such as a dentist or a doctor. Ask for referrals. Check out the physician, program, or therapist's credentials or write-ups in the medical literature. No one program, or doctor, is right for everyone; personality, individual tastes and differences, and costs are all issues that have to be addressed. What matters is that you commit to beginning and staying on a medically approved and supervised weight loss and management program that works for you.

What type of program will work best for you? Take this self-evaluation to find out:

Yes_____No_____

1. Do you need a flexible or fixed program?__________
2. Do you want to prepare all your own meals?________
3. Do you want to work with a doctor, nutritionist, program leader, or therapist?________
4. Do you want to be monitored weekly?________
5. Do you want individual support?________
6. Do you want group support? ________
7. Do you need a program or procedure that is covered by your healthcare insurance? ________
8. Do you want an online program?________
9. Are you under a doctor's care for a medical condition that requires regular monitoring of your diet by a physician? ________
10. Do you have an eating disorder such as compulsive overeating, poor body image, anorexia nervosa, or bulimia? ________

Summary of results. If you answered "yes" to question 1, a structured program that tells you exactly what to eat and also sells the food may be something to consider.

If you answered "yes" to question 2, and you want to prepare all your own meals, a program that encourages food preparation, and even provides recipes, might be better for you.

If you answered "yes" to question 9 that you have a medical condition that requires a physician's supervision, it may be in your best interest to work with a physician, especially someone with expertise in weight issues.

If you answered "yes" to question 10, and you have specific psychological issues surrounding food or body image, it may be preferable for you to work with an individual counselor including a psychologist with training in eating disorders, a nutritionist, a social worker, or being part of a weight loss and maintenance program that includes working with an eating disorder expert.

Please note: The above comments are not endorsements of any specific weight loss programs; they are simply a tool to try to interpret your answers to the self-evaluation quiz that might help you make a choice of program that fits your needs or individual situation/condition. Each individual is unique and you should consult with a physician before starting any weight loss program, on your own or under supervision through a commercial weight loss program/plan, whether or not it includes the purchase of food.

Fifteen Ways to Motivate Yourself to Find the Time to Start a Creative Weight Management Program

Here are fifteen ways to motivate yourself to begin a creative weight management program that will increase the likelihood that you can lose the excess weight that you want to lose and maintain that weight loss while learning new healthier eating and exercise habits:

1. Give yourself a positive affirmation, even something as simple as telling yourself, "I can do it!"
2. Make a list of the reasons you want to lose weight and keep it off. How will your weight loss, and maintenance, benefit

you? Here are some key benefits that you might keep in mind:

- To feel healthier
- To have more energy
- To set a better example for your spouse or children
- To get into clothing that has become too tight, or to fit into an old, favorite outfit
- To increase your self-esteem
- To have less weight on ankles, which may reduce the number of, or likelihood of, varicose veins
- To be able to focus on other personal or professional issues and be able to give up the obsession about being overweight or obese
- To be able to smile when walking by a mirror
- To feel comfortable in a swimsuit
- To feel like more than just "a pretty face"
- To find that rings aren't as tight or that you are able to remove them, if you want to
- To smile at the realization that you're increasing your life expectancy
- To feel proud that you are achieving your weight loss and maintenance goals
- To put the time and energy that you put into overeating or snacking into more productive ways to spend your time, such as taking a walk, reading a book, calling a friend on the phone, writing a letter, or taking up a new hobby
- To have more stamina
- To be able to buy sample sizes at the department store at a reduced cost
- Other reasons (not listed above): ____________________

  ____

  ____

3. Learn from the diets you have been on, and off, in the past,

but put those experiences behind you and start afresh. Think about the last time you tried to lose weight and keep it off. What happened to sabotage your efforts? How can you avoid that happening this time? What are you going to do differently this time that will increase the likelihood that you will succeed?

4. Remember that you need to put yourself, and your health, first. Even if others depend on you, you'll be better equipped at being there for them if you feel good and like how you look.
5. Share with someone you trust your wish to start a weight management program. Pick someone who is positive and supportive. Having someone who cares about you to share in your weight loss and management program may keep you motivated even when the going gets tough.
6. Give yourself permission to stop hating yourself, whatever your weight.
7. Feel good about deciding to work at achieving this very difficult goal.
8. Get on the scale so you know the reality of your current weight.
   Record the weight you are starting at here: ____________
   What is your goal? ____________
   Is that goal realistic? Why have you chosen that particular weight? Does it have meaning for you, whether that's the weight you were when you went to the high school prom, or for your wedding? Is that weight realistic for your current age, frame and activity level?
9. Start keeping track of *everything* you eat as well as when you eat it, and why. (Hunger? Depression? Boredom? Nervousness? Habit?)
10. If you wish, take a "before" picture. You might find it useful to chronicle your weight loss and maintenance progress.

Date ____________

YOUR PICTURE

11. Tell yourself, "I'll give it a try," and take it a meal at a time.
12. Write a list of your priority concerns over the next day. Now rewrite the list and put "begin weight management program" as your number one priority.
13. If you do better under a doctor's care, in a supervised weight management program, working individually with a doctor, nutritionist, or weight counselor, with other peers and a trained leader, or in a self-help discussion group, make an appointment or find out the operating hours for the program and *get there*!
14. Pick rewards for each step of the way that will help to motivate you. It need not be expensive or even meaningful to others. They should be rewards that will motivate *you*. Make a list or create a contract with yourself: "When I lose three pounds, I will…", "When I lose ten pounds, I will…"
15. Think about what will work for *you*. Is it better for you to tell others that you're starting a new diet, or keep it to yourself? Will it motivate you to buy a new pair of pants, a size smaller, and keep it in the closet to motivate you, or will that discourage you instead?

    Think about how you will make this creative management program customized to your needs, desires and strengths. You know yourself better than anyone else knows you. Everything you learn about weight management is a generality. You need to consider how any advice, information or suggestions apply to you.

The Last Straw

"The last straw" is a way of getting motivated to do something as all-consuming as beginning, and sticking with, a weight management program. The last straw is that trigger event or emotion that gets you to the point that you're willing to put in the time and effort to lose the 10, 20, 40, 50, or 100+ pounds that you need to lose and keep off.

Have you reached your last straw about your weight? What have been some of the incidents or comments lately that have made you want to do something about your weight? Use the space below to record those comments or describe those incidents:

____

____

____

____

Maybe you're not at a point of needing to do something yet. That's okay. If you're reading this book, at least you're considering making a change. That's the first step. You may need a last straw to give you the motivation and energy to commit to a weight reduction and management program.

Some begin a weight loss program because of a medical last straw. For example, a friend of mine met with a nutritionist at the hospital, soon after her overweight, 43-year-old husband suffered a minor heart attack. She was given guidelines about her husband's diet. Since following those guidelines, she and her husband have both been losing weight.

Others begin diets because of imminent special occasions, such as a high school reunion, a wedding, or a vacation that will require wearing a bathing suit. That's okay, especially if you stick with your weight reduction and management program even after the special occasion is behind you. However, a study reported in the *Journal of Social Psychology* found that *self-motivation*, not special occasions, was a better predictor of long-term weight reduction and diet success. Those *personal* last straws or triggers just may be the best motivators.

Okay, so you're following the trend of collective last straws, namely, the two key times of the year that new diets are started:

- As a New Year resolution (so the new weight management program traditionally begins on 1 January or the first "back to work day" after the New Year holiday).
- After the summer, when fall begins, with the hope that next summer you *will* want to be seen in a bathing suit and go swimming.

Even if your last straw is something imposed by the calendar, now commit to your new healthier way of eating and living so *self-motivation* kicks in and takes over.

Here is *my* Last Straw that got me to go to Weight Watchers® in June 2010. *I made a short 4-minute movie called* She Tweets *which I co-wrote and co-starred in as part of the "48 Hour Film Project". The following week, when I saw the movie in a screening at NYU, I was surprised by how big I looked on the screen. That motivated me to get on the scale the next morning. I was totally shocked to discover I had gotten to the point of weighing 204 pounds. I knew I had gained some weight, but by wearing stretch pants, I was able to deny to myself just how much weight I had gained. I had at least 60 pounds to lose to get into a healthy range for my height and frame.*

Being Overweight or Obese Is a Health Issue

There has been a movement to just accept yourself as overweight or obese. When I consider the titles of some of the weight-related books at the bookstore, the themes are the same: love yourself at your natural, bigger size; stop dieting. I was even writing a book like that at the point where overcoming my weight problem seemed an impossible task.

However, the related health problems associated with being overweight or obese make it too important an issue to dismiss by saying, "Fine. I'll just accept myself the way I am."

The National Institute of Diabetes and Digestive and Kidney Diseases (NIDDK) estimates the total cost of being overweight and obesity in the US at $117 billion, including $61 billion in diet costs and $56 billion in indirect costs—this is equal to the economic cost of cigarette smoking— and this does not include the $33 billion spent annually in the US on weight-loss products and services.

Employers are paying for these excess expenditures since workers with illnesses related to obesity and being overweight cost more to insure and have more sick days when work is not done or temporary additional workers have to be hired. According to the NIDDK, the costs in lost productivity related to obesity for Americans aged 17–64 is $3.9 billion, which includes lost workdays, physician visits directly tied to obesity, restricted activity days, and days in bed because of obesity-related afflictions.

The US government reports "Do You Know the Health Risks of Overweightness?" and "Statistics Related to Overweight and Obesity" reiterate that health problems are more likely if you are overweight or obese, including heart disease, stroke, diabetes, certain types of cancer, sleep apnea and osteoarthritis (for women, uterus, gallbladder, cervix, ovary, breast, and colon; for men, colon, rectum, and prostate cancer), gallbladder disease, and gout. Obesity is also associated with:

- High blood cholesterol
- Complications of pregnancy
- Menstrual irregularities

- Hirsutism (presence of excess body and facial hair)
- Stress incontinence (urine leakage caused by weak pelvic-floor muscles)
- Depression
- Increased surgical risk

Children Are Getting Fatter Too

One in five American children between the ages of six and seventeen are overweight. In the UK, overweight children have increased from 23 to 28 per cent in an eight-year period. As noted before, Elaine Sciolino points out in her article on the increase of obesity in France that children in France are getting fatter as well.

There are health hazards for children associated with being overweight. For example, as a New Zealand study points out, being overweight increases the likelihood that children will break their bones.

Creative weight management is a family concern. The fact that there are more and more overweight and obese children today is related to the fact that children are first learning their poor eating habits—and sedentary ways—from their parents.

If you need additional motivation to lose weight and keep it off—if doing it for yourself isn't enough to motivate you—then do it for your child or children. They need you to set the right example for them!

It is from your example (among other influences, such as peers and advertising, but yours is primary) that they will learn the food habits that they bring into their teenage and adult years. What we feed our children, as well as our attitudes toward food, will initially be learned from us.

There are numerous causes of obesity and weight gain in children and teens, such as over-consumption of high-calorie junk food, lack of exercise, using food to soothe oneself for stress or anxiety, peer pressure, as well as poor habits. A parent is able to do something about some of those causes. For example, the parent can offer nutritious and delicious meals when a child or teen is eating at home.

But other causes are up to the child or teen to work out, with or without outside help. If outside help is deemed necessary, it is available from a nutritionist, school nurse, physician, therapist or eating disorder expert.

You Can Improve Your Health by Losing As Little As 10 to 20 Pounds

Health columnist Jane E. Brody, reporting in *The New York Times*, based on *The New England Journal of Medicine* study cited above, answers the question, "Just how perilous can 25 extra pounds be?" by noting that Americans now need to realize that "moderately overweight people have long assumed that their main concern was a cosmetic one."

We now know that's just not true. As Brody writes: "Now, it seems, they should be more worried about their health and life expectancy than about how they look."

Exercise Is Crucial

The study, "Body Weight and Mortality Among Women", reported in the *New England Journal of Medicine*, found that in the 115,195 women studied over a 16-year-period confirmed: "Without regular physical activity, weight control can usually not be achieved."

An article in *JAAPA* (*Journal of the American Academy of Physicians Assistants*), "Health Benefits of Exercise", highlights additional reasons for regular exercising, including losing excess fat, helping bones to stay healthy, increasing HDL ("good") cholesterol and lowering LDL ("bad") cholesterol; diminishing feelings of anxiety, depression and stress; reducing the risk of diabetes, colon cancer, breast cancer and heart disease.

Losing Weight, and Keeping It Off, Takes Hard Work

Just as doing well on a test usually requires studying and solid work, losing weight and keeping it off requires effort. Just how much effort will of course vary from person to person. Dieting, and maintaining a weight loss, usually has to be an *obsession*—a *positive* obsession—if you are to achieve your weight goal, and keep it.

Getting on the scale and being within the range of weight that is best for your health and self-esteem is evidence that your weight management is successful.

Achieving the weight you want and maintaining it is, for most of us, even harder than quitting smoking. That's tough, really tough, but once you stop smoking, you need never smoke another cigarette again, ever.

But we all have to eat! We can't stop eating!

Moderation. Ask any workaholic—or former workaholic—and he or she will probably agree that learning to work *in moderation* is far harder than working around the clock with abandon.

For those of us with a weight problem, we have to learn healthier and more effective ways of eating. That's usually more challenging than giving something up completely.

What we all want to do is eat balanced meals—like having a balanced life, not one that is all work or all play—not starving or bingeing, dieting intensely only to have a rebound effect whereby we regain what we lost, and finding ourselves weighing even more than when we started.

Failing Toward Success

There's another message behind this book: we all fail as we head towards success! Don't beat yourself up if you've tried to lose weight and maintain a recommended weight for yourself once, twice, or many more times and failed. You will get it right! Each time you tackle this issue you learn something more about yourself and food. There's a lot of controversy about whether or not yo-yo dieting is bad for you. The research swings back and forth between saying, it's worse to lose weight, and regain it than it is to stay consistently overweight. Check with your doctor or healthcare professional about the most current thinking on that issue.

You need to be positive and optimistic that *this time* you *will* succeed because you're trying a new strategy—perhaps you're keeping a weight management journal, trying a different medically sound, supervised program, taking classes in low-fat or lower-calorie cooking or nutrition, seeing a therapist, or just trying to have new and different insights into overeating and the whole process of dieting. Maybe you are more likely to achieve your weight loss and maintenance goals this time because you are older and wiser now, or maybe you've actually learned something from all the other diets you've been on before that worked, or failed, to a certain degree. Maybe you are starting to have shortness of breath when you try to walk up the stairs, or you are beginning to believe the statistics about how being overweight or obese increases the likelihood that you will have a heart attack, and this is the *last straw*—you are finally motivated to get focused and lose weight and stay healthy.

You Are Learning a Whole New Approach to Eating and Exercise

Gaining control over your weight problem is a continual reeducation process. You probably didn't get overweight or obese overnight or even in a few days, weeks, or months. It's going to take time to unlearn your old, negative habits and learn some positive new ones. It will take time to get a grip on this weight challenge.

Think back to when you learned to drive a car. You took lessons. You practised. One day it all came together and you were able to drive without a teacher next to you. But it may have been a while before you were completely confident about your driving. The same process will come into play as you rethink your eating, dieting, weight loss, weight loss maintenance, and exercise strategy, and as you develop a new *creative weight management* program that works for you.

But whatever your motivation to get started, pat yourself on the back for getting started! It's a big step; applaud yourself for taking it.

Hopefully you're all charged up and ready to start a weight management program, to learn healthier eating habits and to look at exercise in a more positive way. You'll find some tips to help you along the way in the next chapter, "Day One, How People Change, and Planning for Success". Good luck as you begin this new, completely fresh Day One!

7

DAY ONE, HOW PEOPLE CHANGE AND PLANNING FOR SUCCESS

You're taking the next step! You're starting a new creative weight management program that includes a plan to lose weight, exercise, and maintain your weight loss and preferred weight. You are taking the time—making the time—to get on *The Fast Track Guide to Losing Weight and Keeping It Off.* You may be doing it under the care of a physician, following the guidelines provided by a nutritionist, or as part of a medically approved and supervised weight reduction program. As long as you are on a healthy diet that is not a "fad" or "fast" diet, that's fine. You need to find the weight loss and management program or plan that works best for you.

The bottom line is that you are approaching that moment you commit to change: Day One.

The key is to consider the gift you are giving yourself, and your family, as the gift of healthy eating—not as a diet. A diet is something you go on, and go off. No, this is a new way of approaching food. Initially, if you have to lose weight, you will be on the reducing phase of this new way of embracing food.

But once you reach your goal weight, you will maintain your weight loss, and form new habits, rather than reverting to the old ones (and the weight gain that accompanied those habits).

There has to be a Day One to your changes, a starting point. This Day One is the beginning of showing, through your actions, that what you put into your mouth is as important as how you spend your money, the choices you make about what movie to see, what vacation spot you'll go to with your family, the friends you'll visit or call, the books you'll read, the community you choose to live in, the car you choose to buy, the job or career you are pursuing, and who you will vote for in the next election.

All the little decisions about food that you make each and every day add up. You're either thrilled with your choices or regretful and disappointed.

Day One

Doesn't that have a nice ring to it?

Have you picked a goal weight that is realistic for your height, body frame, age, and activity level?

Get on the scale, if you like, and record your starting weight on a sheet of paper or in your journal, such as the *Time to Lose Journal*, if you're keeping one.

How often will you weigh yourself? Every day? Once a week? Twice a week? If you are following a supervised weight-management program with a weekly weigh in, you may wish to only weigh in when you go to your physician, nutritionist, or attend the program. You may find that once a week, at the same time of day, with the same type of clothes, with or without shoes, as long as you're consistent, is the ideal way of judging how you do from week to week.

Some may find that the way a pair of pants or a dress fits is the sign that progress is being made in the right direction. Others may have to weigh-in daily to get a more concrete way of finding out about their progress. But if you are following the program that you have chosen, even if there are some small day-to-day fluctuations, overall you should be going in the direction that you want to go in.

Remember that you're going to take it a day, even a meal, at a time. You didn't get overweight or obese in a day. You're not going to lose the weight, and maintain it, in a day.

The key to creative weight management is the idea that this is a renewed and healthier way of approaching food, dieting, and maintaining your preferred weight. Rather than becoming a slave to the scale or obsessed with food and calories, you are simply considering the nutritional value of everything you eat and how it fits in with your program. Just as you consider what you spend your money on so you stay within your budget, you are considering your food intake so you stay within the guidelines of whatever program you have chosen to follow.

Here's a poem I wrote about focusing on just one day at a time. I find it helpful to reread it from time to time, when the going gets tough on my weight loss and ideal weight maintenance journey. I hope you find it helpful as well:

Just For Today

Just for today I'll try my best
Just for today.

Just for today
I'll focus on now and not the rest
Just for today.

Just for today
I'll count my blessing.
Just for today
I'll count my fingers and my toes.

Just for today
I'll think of someone less fortunate.
Just for today
I'll hug those I love.

Just for today
I'll look at the bright side.
Just for today
I'll think of all that I've achieved.

Just for today
I'll try not to complain as much.

Just for today.
Just for today.

Why not try to write your own poem or, if just free associating and writing whatever you what is more comfortable for you, just write down your thoughts about your Day One. Use your journal, a separate piece of paper or, if you wish, use the space below.

Today's date ______________________________

My Thoughts About Day One

____
____
____
____
____
____

Creative Weight Management Principle #4:

Be prepared. *Plan, shop, and prepare for each meal or snack.*

Checklist for Day One

1. **Picking Your Day One:** The first step for optimizing the success of Day One is picking the right day. For me, it was the Monday after my husband Fred and I returned from our week away in Florida. We decided during that week not to be concerned about "watching" what we were eating. We had both put on many pounds since we had stopped going to the weekly meetings of the formal weight plan we had decided to stop following. But we also knew we did not want to have to think about dieting during our trip.

Even before we left on our trip, Fred and I discussed our commitment to starting a new plan upon our return. I even made the appointment at the program we were now going to follow. It was comforting to have made that commitment and to have that Day One in our appointment books.

If you tend to be an emotional eater for one or more reasons, especially because of stress, pressure, or anxiety, you may also want to select as your Day One for this new creative weight management program a day that is better for you in terms of what is going on with your personal life or your career. The night before the final exam at college, the first day on a new job, or the first day of your family vacation may not be the ideal time to begin a new creative weight management program.

On the other hand, there are some events that can be an excellent motivator: your upcoming wedding or a high school reunion. If those dates are far enough in advance that you can make some realistic progress in your weight loss goals, depending upon how much you have to lose, let's say anywhere from a month or two to, preferably, four to six months or longer in the future, you might find those events inspire you to make positive changes rather than put pressure on you that backfires and sends you further into overeating.

However, you do not want to become a perfectionist in your search for the ideal time to begin Day One. Just keep in mind that trying to minimize or eliminate emotional eating may initially take its toll on you as you learn new ways to channel those feelings as well as non-food ways to deal with those emotions.

2. **Picking a Plan:** As you know, there is no one way to lose weight and keep it off, but you do need a plan.

   Part of Day One is deciding on your plan.

   Ask yourself these questions: Have I had a check-up

at the doctor's to get an "okay" to start a weight loss plan? If not, when will I schedule that appointment? Once you have chosen the plan you will follow, think, am I thoroughly familiar with the plan? If not, when will I take the time to review the plan again or call someone who could help explain it to me?

3. **Preparing Your Environment for Your Day One:** Keeping with the underlying theme of *The Fast Track Guide to Losing Weight and Keeping It Off,* in terms of planning for your success, what actions will you take to help increase your success on Day One? To help your creative weight management program's success, you need to do whatever works for *you.*

   Do you function better if you get rid of all the foods in your house or apartment that cause you to lose control—the socalled "trigger" foods—or is it better to have those foods around so you can say "no" to them? I used to throw out all my trigger foods before I began a diet. I remember back in college my friends in the dormitory used to joke about it because I had a ritual of eating anything I wanted late at night, but then at the stroke of midnight, I threw out all the junk food, resolving to start my diet the next day.

   Now, I find it more empowering to have the "trigger" foods around because I have learned to eat in moderation. So I don't just have some candy around, I have lots and lots of candy, but I only have one piece a day.

   If you are a diabetic even one piece of candy is not allowed; for health or even psychological reasons, having a daily piece of candy is not for everyone. Always check with your physician if you have particular health conditions, such as diabetes.

   Do you have all the foods you need on hand or do you need to go to the supermarket for fresh fruit and vegetables?

   Here are some additional questions to ask yourself:

1. If I need to eliminate having any "trigger" foods around, have I gone through my refrigerator and pantry getting rid of anything that I think will sabotage my weight management program?
2. Have I gone food shopping for everything I need for the food plan that I have chosen to follow for today, tomorrow, and as many days as I want to shop for in advance?
3. Have I decided on a target goal weight that is realistic for me?
4. Have I decided when, where, and how often I will weigh myself, or weigh in?
5. If I want to take a "Before" picture, have I done it?
6. What are the strategies I will follow for this new healthy eating and weight management plan? Will I tell others about it, or keep it to myself? Will I try to find a partner to diet along with me, or do it on my own?
7. Just as I would do with a to-do list at work or a shopping list for going to the grocery store, have I developed a list of everything I need to do to make this Day One successful for me and checked off each item as I completed those actions?

You may find it helpful to take an inventory of your personality as well as of your home or office environment, and figure out how you can optimize the likelihood that you will succeed on your weight loss and management program. Just like the skydiver who meticulously checks and rechecks his or her parachute gear before jumping out of that plane, you need to find or buy yourself all the foods or condiments, like spices for adding flavor to your foods, or tools, such as measuring spoons or cups, as well as preparing yourself mentally for this weight battle.

Here are some helpful weight loss and maintenance aids to consider having available to help you with your healthy eating regime:

Equipment

Food scale

Measuring cups

¼ cup size

½ cup size

1 cup size

2 cup size

Measuring spoons

1 tablespoon

1 teaspoon

½ teaspoon

¼ teaspoon

Cooking utensils

Different size pots and pans for cooking and baking

Storage containers (for storage in the refrigerator, freezer, and/or reheating in the microwave)

Non-stick spray for sautéing/cooking without butter or oil

Other:

Spices

Note: If any food listed is not available in your area, substitute different foods that are comparable and that work for you and your diet challenge.

Chef Paul Prudhomme's® Magic Seasoning Blends®

Condiments, including parsley flakes, basil leaves, garlic powder

Beverages

Water

Zero- or low-calorie flavored drinks available in your area

Here are several foods that work for me when I get the munchies—but remember I am not a nutritionist or dietician, I am a health writer/researcher and a time management and relationship consultant. Do not add anything to your own weight program without consulting with your supervised weight counselor/leader:

- Salsa (regular or Mango)
- Low-calorie ice pops (sugar-free, just 15 calories per ice pop)
- Raw or canned vegetables including:
  - String beans (canned)—You can get sodiumreduced if you are concerned about the high sodium content of some canned goods
  - Peppers (green or red)
  - Celery
  - Lettuce
  - Cauliflower
  - Cabbage
  - Brussels sprouts
- ______________________________
- ______________________________

What other low- or zero-calorie foods help you, and do you want to have available, when or if you get emotional rather than physical hunger, and you need something to nibble on?

What are some other foods that will help you get through your own weight program? Make a list of what you need and make it a priority to get those foods and have ample supplies. If perishable, make sure you replenish regularly.

How People Change

Therapist Allen Wheelis, in his book titled *How People Change*, wrote about suffering. He argued that suffering could be caused by something physical, like being in prison or starvation or by something mental. Both types of suffering are just as real to the sufferer.

"Who is ultimately responsible for change?" asks Wheelis. The individual. Even psychotherapists are only the catalyst for change.

This is a key idea, an extension of the notion in Chapter 3, "Overcoming Blocks to Successful Creative Weight Management", where there was a discussion of neither blaming others for your own failures nor crediting others solely for your success. You want to empower yourself by praising yourself for your weight loss and management success, and neither applaud nor blame others for your changes so that you take full responsibility for your efforts and your success.

How do you accomplish change?

There is a debate over whether you need to change how you think first, causing different actions to follow; or whether you need to modify your actions, thereby changing your thinking.

Both ways are actually true; both ways work. At different points in your life, with varied tasks or individuals, you may find you bring about change by doing varied actions; only in time does your thinking also change. By contrast, you may find you are unable to take a distinctive course of action without *first* changing your thinking.

As noted before, my friend whose husband's heart attack was the last straw for both of them to change their eating habits has been following the same low-fat, low-sugar, lowcalorie, low-cholesterol diet sanctioned by his doctor and nutritionist. She's been following it for the last six weeks. She still brings cookies and fat-free doughnuts into the house for her three sons, who are all slim. "I look at the cookies now and I don't even want them," she told me.

That's a wonderful way to change one's response to cookies—from within!

You are what you do! You are what you think! You are what you eat!

In *How People Change*, Wheelis writes about how the idea

of "we are what we do" translates into how we change. If you substitute the words overeating or bingeing for the character traits he's writing about, you have an excellent idea of how to transform yourself from an overeater to someone who is creatively and successfully managing your eating and weight.

"Personality change follows change in behavior," writes Wheelis. "Since we are what we do, if we want to change what we are, we must begin by changing what we do, [and] undertake a new mode of action."

As Wheelis and other psychologists have pointed out, if you perform an action often enough, you will integrate that action so that it becomes second nature. If you substitute positive eating habits for negative ones and do it long enough, those habits will also become as familiar as the previous ones.

But it all begins with Day One. In order to change, you have to take that first step, start with Day One, followed by Day Two, Day Three, Day Twenty-one, Day Fifty, and you are more likely to see those changes becoming permanent changes because of the consistency and frequency with which you are reinforcing those efforts.

Positive Image About How You Want to Change

In order to achieve a new you, in order to get to Day One, you might find it useful to create a positive image of how you want to look, the eating habits you want to have, and the exercise program you want to practise. As the late esteemed career counselor John Crystal said in an interview, "Part of what we've been teaching people over the years is [that] nobody's going to give you what you want if you don't even know what it is yourself."

Positive image on what you want for your weight and your size.

My goal in this chapter is to psyche you up, so you start making that positive image into your new reality.

I want to inspire you so you get yourself to the point that you are ready for your Day One.

I feel very enthusiastic about this! From my own experience, I know that the world looks different to me, and I feel so much more energetic since I lost 60.2 excess pounds. When I go through airports or any public place where I see countless people, and I observe severely overweight or obese men or women, I want to run up to them and say, "You don't have to be overweight! You don't have to be obese! You don't have to shorten your life and increase the likelihood of such illnesses as diabetes, cancer or heart disease. You can make such a difference in your health and in your appearance if you lose those extra pounds."

I want to say that to perfect strangers, but I don't. I just think it.

But I can write it and share those thoughts with you. Because you're reading this book, I know you're receptive to the ideas that I'm sharing.

I know that you're ready to give yourself a Day One.

Maybe not today.

Maybe not tomorrow.

Maybe you need to read this book and put it aside until you have a Last Straw to motivate you to do the hard and consistent work that losing weight, and keeping it off, requires.

But I'm there for you until you have Day One, and once you start on your path of renewal.

I'm there for you because I am sharing one of the biggest secrets today. The secret is that *few people can maintain their ideal weight without effort.*

They may not want to admit that to you.

We live in a society that applauds success as if it was meant to be.

But it requires concerted effort, and yet few will want to hear about the daily, even hourly, decisions you need to make to keep yourself on the right path.

You're not alone in this struggle!

Begin Day One, stay committed, and you *will* reach your goal weight and maintain that ideal weight.

Yes, it's going to take a long time for all the healthier habits you're trying to establish for yourself (and your family) to become second nature. You've probably been overeating, grabbing anything and everything in sight, for a long time. Considering what you eat—how much of it and how often—is going to take time for it to become second nature.

Furthermore, it will take many meals and days for you to get where you want to be and to learn how to stay at that ideal or goal weight. You will not be "perfect". As you've seen in Chapter 4, "Dealing with the Psychological and Sociological Aspects of Overeating and Weight Challenges", perfectionism is counterproductive to your weight management efforts. So you've got to be kind to yourself if and when you have an occasional "slip". As Wheelis points out, it's not the one or two times you go "off the wagon" that will define you and your efforts, but your overall orientation to what you eat. Are you a creative weight manager? Are you managing what you eat, and how you approach food, or is food in control of you?

Every Day Is Day One

You may need an official Day One to begin your creative weight management program. But what's working for me is that I see *every day* as a new Day One. Even today, this morning, I woke up and recommitted myself to my creative weight management principles and actions. I know that by continuing to put into practise the principles shared in this book, in time and with effort, I will lose my remaining three pounds and get to my goal weight of 139.

Whether it's the first day of your "diet" or creative weight management program, the second, the 20th, the 240th, or you've reached your ideal weight and you're now maintaining your weight, consider every day as Day One of your creative weight management program. It will help to keep you focused in the now and not in the past or the future.

Setting Goals

A key time management principle is to set goals, reasonable goals. As I noted in *Creative Time Management for the New Millennium*, by setting goals and directing yourself towards that goal, you have a path to follow. It will also be a clear measure that you have achieved your goal.

Long-term Goals

We use goal setting at school and then in business to help prioritize actions and to measure achievements.

In terms of your weight loss and maintenance goals, at least initially, you will probably want to have a number on the scale for your long-term goal—a number or a size. That's fine. That's the way, for better or worse, we measure how we fit our own standards (as well as the society's) of what we should weigh or the size we should wear.

But in addition to that number on the scale or the size you want to wear, hopefully you will set a long-term goal that involves eating a different way or making regular exercise a part of your everyday regime.

The number long-term goal could be expressed this way: "I want to weigh ________."

That's an important number to decide on. What is the preferred weight to aim for based on your height, body type, and activity level? Another way to determine your ideal weight is to compute your BMI—Body Mass Index. The U.S. Government provides a calculator that you can use to compute your current and preferred BMI at this website/URL: http://nhlbisupport.com/bmi. It will also let you know what the BMI categories are for being underweight, normal weight, overweight, or obese.

Another way to pick a preferred weight is to consider when, over your lifetime, you looked the way you most want to look, and what your weight was at that time. There may be mitigating factors that require that you adjust your weight up or down from that number, such as activity level and any other factors that render that number not applicable today.

There is also the challenge of the psychological or sociological meaning behind a number that might impact whether or not a number is a realistic goal today. For example, one of the survey respondents to my weight history survey is a 25-year-old single freelance writer whom I'll call Gloria. Gloria is 5'6", and she currently weighs 123 pounds. How many readers are thinking: "What a perfect weight! She must have quite a figure. I wish I could weigh 123 pounds!"

Alas, Gloria checked off both of these statements: "I am currently on a diet to lose weight", and "I have been on a diet within the last year". She also shared that "I would like to lose five pounds".

The first reason Gloria wants to lose five pounds is related to her exercise goal. She notes: "Now that I'm going to start distance running, I want to lose some more fat—I don't want to drag it around."

But Gloria wants to weigh 120 pounds or less. The secondary reason she wants to lose five pounds may have to do with this telling anecdote from her formative years that she shared with me:

> I also have a connection to the number: 120 pounds. This is an awful story, but true: when I was, oh, maybe 15, I was down the shore with my family. It was me, my mom, grandmom and dad in the room. We were talking about weight or something, and they asked how much I weighed.

> I said 125. My dad said "That's 5 pounds too much." We all stared at him, shocked that he would say that. I was in pretty good shape, a high school athlete. "Well, 120 is the perfect weight for a woman. You're fine, Gloria. I'm not saying you're fat." Ugh. I think it's still with me.

I have a similar "number in my head" story, but it's far less dramatic than Gloria's. However, you might find it useful as a consideration when you set your own preferred weight goal: is it a realistic number?

Until recently, I used to have the number of 132 in my head as my preferred weight. I'm 5'6", and I would want to be 132 because that's what I weighed as a junior in high school. I still have the image of myself in that strapless white prom dress that my Grandmother and I picked out, and I was the belle of the ball—the high school cheerleader on the arm of the high school basketball hero.

When I've lost weight in the past, I would drive myself in an unrealistic way to try to get to 132. Instead of getting there, as my frustration mounted, I would start going back up the scale!

That is why this time I set a much more realistic preferred weight as my goal: 145. I'm already a size 6 and my BMI is within the normal range according to the US government charts.

We all get these numbers in our head, whether it's the number we want to see on the scale or the size we want to see on our clothes. It can really impact how we "see" ourselves; be careful to pick a number that is realistic—achievable and desirable. You can, of course, also create a tentative weight goal that you reevaluate when you are closer to that goal, adjusting it up or down on your own or in discussion with your physician, nutritionist or weight program leader.

So in addition to that number or that size, use the space below to set one or more long-term goals that you will also be working towards, such as, "I want to learn how to control what I eat and when I eat without feeling deprived." "I want to be able to lose weight and still eat chocolate every day." That was my long-term goal for this program that's working, and I'm pleased to report that I've achieved this goal! Another possible long-term goal: "I want to work out for 30 minutes every day and find it enjoyable, rather than something to be dreaded."

Use the space below, or make notes in your smartphone, computer, or a piece of paper, to write down your long-term goals beside the number or size that you indicated above:

1. ______________________________
2. ______________________________
3. ______________________________

Remember some of the key components to a goal that will motivate you and help you achieve your goal, rather than overwhelm or frustrate you: make the goal something that is specific and that can be measured. If you write your long-term goal as "I want to exercise", that is harder to work towards, and measure, than something specific, such as "I want to exercise three times a week varying my workout from the treadmill and outdoor running to bicycle riding and swimming, with each session lasting 30 minutes."

Short-term Goals

Now that you have your long-term goals, you want to figure out your short-term goals. If you just have "I want to lose 50 pounds" as your goal, you can get frustrated very quickly when you find you have only lost a pound or two, and it seems so hard and far until you reach your long-term goal.

Short-term goals can be achieved in a weekly weigh in. Measure how much weight you have lost within one week; if you are "losing" with others in a program or a group, your successes will be applauded, and any weight gains could be discussed and analyzed. Sometimes understanding why someone gained one or more pounds during the week can be as much, or more, of a learning experience than why someone had a "good" week and lost 1–3 pounds.

I like to get on the scale daily, in addition to my weekly weigh-ins, to keep myself more aware of how certain meals or foods impact on my weight. But this is a personal preference, and everyone has to find the appropriate frequency that he or she gets on the scale, or even if the scale will be used at all, instead of how clothes fit, or taking measurements with a tape measure.

In addition to monitoring weekly weight losses, another short-term goal is to get through each day. For some, including me, it is to get through each meal and each time period between the meals.

Here are a few samples of short-term goals to consider for yourself:

"Today I will stay within the range of the program that I am following."

"I will get to the gym for 20 minutes today."

"I will write down everything I'm eating today, including snacks."

"I will drink X number of glasses of water today." (Check with your physician and/or medically-sound supervised program for the recommended number of glasses of water to drink every day.)

"I will make my weight loss and maintenance program my number one priority, putting the time and effort into creating daily and weekly menu plans, shopping lists, as well as putting the time and effort into buying prepared foods or preparing the foods that will help me to achieve my goal."

Now use the space below to write your short-term weight goals:

1. ________________________________
2. ________________________________
3. ________________________________

Reminder: Take the Time to Learn Your Program Inside and Out

Take the time to learn what your program offers you. The more familiar you are with the program, the more likely you will get the most out of it. Read any written materials that your physician, nutritionist, or program leader has provided. Ask questions if you are unclear about anything.

We noted earlier that boredom could be a block to losing and maintaining weight loss. Help fight boredom by sharing information, such as recipes or tips for making the program more interesting or easy to follow, with others who are following the same plan. If you are following the program on your own, see if there are any cookbooks you can find to offer suggestions for making the program meals tasty and easier to follow.

Keep the information about the program you are on handy. You might keep a pocket version in your handbag or briefcase. You could keep a longer or more expanded version in a file folder or in a loose-leaf binder.

From Day One to Day Twenty-one

It starts with Day One, and then a new habit forms by continuing the next day, and the next, and the next, until, *voilà*, within a couple of weeks the old negative habits are replaced with new positive ones.

Of course it's not as simple as that, but it is the consistency of trying new habits that helps to reinforce those new ways.

The common thinking is that you can see some dramatic permanent changes if you keep at a new positive habit for 21 days. As noted before, this theory is based on Dr Maxwell Maltz' classic book, *Psychocybernetics,* in which Dr Maltz had observed that someone who lost a limb took 21 days to no longer perceive the limb as being there.

The 21-day concept has clicked with many people, and some of us feel that if we can only make it to three weeks, we have a greater likelihood to making those positive changes into permanent ones. If thinking in terms of 21 days instead of "forever" is helpful to you, great! I have personally found that even getting through one complete week doing things differently helps me to get to week two, and then week three, and beyond.

8

FIFTY ALTERNATIVES TO OVEREATING

Learning to Turn to Something Besides Food

In addition to dealing with the painful feelings that may be brought up when you stop misusing food to deal with those feelings is the strategy of finding other, non-food ways to help you cope when you are feeling stressed, bored, lonely, angry, depressed, rejected, fearful, or guilty.

You will see listed below fifty ways to deal with these and similar painful or challenging feelings besides overeating. Add as many additional ways that have worked, or might work, for you if those ways are missing from this list.

Fifty Non-food Ways to Deal with What's Going on Inside of You

1. Call or text a friend.
2. Visit a friend, relative, or neighbor.
3. Call a neighbor.
4. Jump rope.
5. Read poetry.
6. Write poetry.
7. Take a walk. Be careful to exercise caution with this suggestion if it's late at night and/or you live in an area in which you should be walking with someone else you trust, not alone.
8. Organize your files; sorting, sifting and rereading clipped articles or old letters.

9. Ask a friend, a child, your spouse or partner to go for a walk with you.
10. Write a letter, send an e-mail or a card, to an old friend.
11. Have fun with clay, creating something with your hands.
12. Watch an exercise show or download an exercise video from youtube.com and follow it.
13. Watch a movie.
14. Watch TV.
15. Use your camcorder, camera or smartphone to make videos of your family, friends or pets.
16. Hug your pet.
17. Take your dog for a walk.
18. Brush your cat's hair, if your cat enjoys that, or pet your cat.
19. Clean something you've been meaning to clean, perhaps the stove, a lighting fixture, the bathtub or the kitchen floor.
20. Rearrange a closet, sorting your clothes by size, gathering together clothing you have not worn in 5 or 10 years and no longer want to wear, regardless of the size. Consider donating those clothes or selling online or in a tag sale.
21. Go bicycle riding.
22. Find and read any old poems or letters you wrote in previous years.
23. Go online and become part of a chat group or a list of people who share your interests or concerns.
24. Hug your partner.
25. Kiss your partner.
26. Make love with your partner.
27. Get a back rub or give a back rub.
28. Listen to a non-fiction or fiction book.
29. Get a massage.
30. Get a facial.
31. Go to a sauna.

32. Go swimming.
33. Play tennis, squash, or ping pong.
34. Go roller-skating or ice skating.
35. Plan a family or friends' reunion.
36. Make a list of all the birthdays you want to remember during the year.
37. Call your sister, brother or cousin.
38. Make a to-do list of professional, career, or educational goals for the next week.
39. Make a to-do list of personal goals for the next week. (Try to keep it to a manageable number of goals, no more than your top three goals in either category that you might be able to achieve.)
40. Take a course on the Internet.
41. Go to your local library and read a book or borrow one.
42. Go to the movies.
43. Go to the theatre or to a comedy club or live music venue.
44. Go to an art museum or gallery.
45. Do volunteer work at a local charity.
46. Tutor someone in an area of your expertise.
47. Go hiking (preferably with someone so you can help each other and communicate along the way).
48. Read the instructions on equipment you've bought that you never got around to reading.
49. Sew on all the buttons and do all the sewing repair jobs you've been meaning to do for months or even years.
50. Go to the mall or to your favorite store. (But be careful not to overspend, substituting for emotional eating a new compulsive, emotional spending, that can have dire consequences on your finances.)

Use the space below to write down other ways you plan to (or already) deal with stress, boredom, anger, frustration, or loneliness besides overeating that are not on the above list:

____

____

____

Losing weight and keeping it off offers an opportunity to learn different non-food ways to deal with stress and other emotions that may be at the root of non-hunger emotional eating that may have led to your weight gain.

But What If Eating Is the "Only" Way to Soothe Yourself?

If the above fifty or more ways just won't do it for you and you just have to eat—overeat, compulsively eat, or eat only out of habit and when you are not hungry—once you are on your weight program, try to minimize the damage you do to your efforts by making better food choices. For example, eating a bowl of string beans, drinking a glass of water, or eating a portion or two of low-calorie gelatin when you have an attack of the munchies will set you back a lot less than a bowl of chocolate fudge ice cream or an entire cake. *Always check with your physician, or your weight loss counselor or nutritionist, before you add any specific foods to your own weight loss and maintenance plan.*

Since we have seen that poor planning is one of the blocks to successful creative weight management, plan ahead for any bouts of uncontrolled overeating that you might have by asking your healthcare or weight-loss professional to provide you with a list of lowcalorie or healthy snack alternatives to high-calorie or high-fat foods that could do more damage to your weight loss and maintenance goals.

Make a list of low-calorie options that you can turn to if you need to eat or drink even if you are not hungry:

9

KEEPING TRACK BY WRITING IN A JOURNAL

Creative Weight Management Principle #5:

Keep track *of what you're eating or snacking on or drinking every day.*

Just as keeping track of what you have to do by creating a to-do list helps to control how you spend your time, keeping track of what you eat and drink on a daily basis helps you stay in control—and in reality, about what you are eating or drinking. Like the todo list in time management, you start off with the plan for the day that your doctor, nutritionist, or weight program leader has recommended that you follow. Then, you use your journal to keep track of what you actually do that day, checking off what you have eaten or had to drink (alternatively, writing down what you are eating or drinking). Either way, the reason for keeping this journal is the same: accountability.

Writing in a journal helps focus your creative weight management efforts on the key principle of breaking up a large, complex, time-consuming, and seemingly overwhelming task, such as losing 5, 7, 10, 25, 50 or 100 or more pounds, into smaller steps or tasks that are usually more manageable, such as losing one pound at a time, or just getting through one day.

Keeping a journal of what you are eating, or what you are feeling, on a daily basis is a way to concretely focus on one meal, one hour, or one day.

A journal offers you the opportunity of concretizing your weight loss and maintenance journey by allowing you to write it down and to break up a complex task into more manageable smaller steps.

Writing May Be a Positive Outlet for Your Emotions

Writing in a journal may also help you to understand why you overeat or turn to food to deal with your emotions. Keeping a journal is not a substitute for a therapist, if professional help is necessary for you to deal with your weight challenge, but it could be used as an additional tool for self-discovery.

The act of writing, and reflecting, could take some of the energy you were putting into eating, or overeating, and focus it on other activities, namely writing.

You may wish to keep your journals completely private, or you may want to share some, or your entire journal with others. That is up to you. The powerful benefits of keeping a journal are manifest in the actual process of writing.

Journals Can Be Used to Manage Your Weight the Way Organizers Are Used to Manage Your Time

Writing down what I was eating, as well as planning out meals, especially the family dinners, helped me when I went shopping for the foods that would keep me on track with my weight loss program.

A journal offers the perfect place to consistently plan what you will cook, as well as what you need to buy at the store. Having a central place to decide on the meals for a day or for a week will probably encourage you to manage your meals in a more active, controlled way.

Keeping a Journal May Help You Stay Motivated

I know when I previously began a weight management program, I needed as much cheering on as possible. Fortunately, the various weight counselors I'd been working with provided that support for me. My husband, family members, and close friends also encouraged me, but I needed to find a way to cheer myself on as well. Keeping a journal helped me to stay motivated and on track. Because of how helpful I found it to be, I created *The Time to Lose Journal*; to accompany this book, I have now created another journal that is called *The 3-Month Food and Exercise Tracker & Journal*. It helps you to keep track of everything you eat and all the exercising you are doing, by writing it down in one central place. It also provides a place to record your thoughts, feelings, and even the "triggers" to any overeating.

But you could use any journal to keep track of your thoughts and weight-related meal plans or weigh-ins, as well as just writing it down on lined paper or using a handheld electronic organizer or laptop or an app.

Like so many, my weight problem did not occur overnight, nor would it be conquered overnight. Depending on your age or how long you have had a weight challenge, you, like me, may have lost 5, 10, 20, 30, 50, 100, or more pounds, not once but many times over. Since beginning this most recent weight loss and maintenance program, which began in June 2004, as I lost more than 60.2 pounds, and kept it off over the next year and a half, I have used keeping a journal as a way to stay motivated as well as to keep on track, regularly recording what I ate, my challenges for that day, as well as using the journal to plan menus for the next week, so I could shop as efficiently as possible.

Writing Down What You Eat May Help You Stay on Your Program

Recording what you eat in a journal may help you to stay on your creative weight management program, especially during the holidays or during particularly stressful times when being aware of what you are eating, or snacking, is even harder.

Psychologists Raymond C. Baker, Ph.D. and Daniel S. Kirschenbaum, Ph.D. monitored 38 dieters during the holidays (Thanksgiving, Hanukah, Christmas, and New Year's Eve). As reported in the July 1998 issue of the American Psychological Association's *Health Psychology*, the researchers found that those dieters who wrote in a journal, recording all the food they ate, as well as the calories in those foods, had better control over their weight during the holidays than those who did not keep a journal.

Writing Down Everything You Eat or Drink Can Help You Get a Grip on "Grazing"

"Grazing" is the term used to describe the out-of-control eating that can lead to weight gain or not losing any weight. You may think you are staying on your program, but you are "grazing", or snacking out of control, and almost unconsciously.

Keeping a journal helps you deal with grazing by making the unconscious conscious; the act of writing down what you are eating or drinking forces you to look at how much you are consuming, and when.

For instance, recently I had an attack of the munchies. I forced myself to write down every single thing I ate, no matter how small. I was surprised, when I added up all the "low-cal" grazings, that I had actually gone over my specified food limit for the day. That is important information for me to have as I continue to get to know myself better through my pro-active creative weight management efforts.

Keeping a Journal May Expand Your Creativity

I have been keeping journals since I was ten years old (although my first journals, I used to call the diaries "Di", and even addressed those bound books as "Dear Di"). Because I have always enjoyed writing, keeping a journal has been a natural extension of my need to express myself. Even when I've been blocked on something I had to write professionally, writing in my journal about being blocked helped me to get through that and complete the professional writing task at hand.

Numerous writers have pointed to the benefits of keeping a journal as a source of inspiration or even as a place to keep notes for poems, short stories, novels, outlines for books, or references that may find their way into a current or future writing project.

But keeping a journal isn't just for professional writers. Indeed, it offers so many emotional, creative, school, and even organizational benefits to all who pick up pen or pencil and record their feelings, thoughts, experiences, notes, ideas, or even bits of dialogue or descriptions to refer back to.

Some Additional Reasons to Keep a Journal

Still wondering if you should take the time to keep a journal? Here are other reasons for keeping a creative weight management journal:

- As a way to reduce stress.
- As a daily outlet for your ideas, feelings, thoughts, and experiences.
- As a regular time and place to allow yourself the chance for reflection.
- As a place to work through a problem such as your weight challenges.

- As a record of your weight management activities and thoughts, for you or for posterity.
- As an opportunity to work on your writing skills including a place to write poetry, short stories, the outline for an article or non-fiction book as well as a place to record observations, dialogue, impressions for possible use later on in creative projects.
- As a fun activity you can do by yourself and for yourself.

10

MAKING PROGRESS TOWARDS YOUR GOAL

Creative Weight Management Principle #6:

Create manageable goals, *rewarding yourself as you go down the scale, as you lose the next smaller unit of weight of the total you have to lose, such as each 1, 3, 5 or 10 pound loss.*

You get on a diet, so that means you also get off it. Unfortunately, that approach to weight management has probably caused you to go up and down, and up, the scale.

Eliminate the Word "Diet" from Your Vocabulary

Erase the notion of a diet and substitute *creative weight management* as a concept.

Instead of a "diet", you are learning a whole new approach to eating and weight management.

You are taking it a day at a time, even a meal or a snack at a time.

If you keep following the medically sound, supervised program that has been recommended for you, you will continue towards your goal whether it takes days, weeks, months, or even years to achieve your preferred weight.

In a previous chapter I dealt with perfectionism and how pivotal it is for you to accept yourself and your imperfections, especially as it relates to reaching your weight goals. When working on losing weight, practically everyone will have an imperfect day on a weight management program. But instead of beating yourself up for being imperfect, you want to get right back on your program, instead of abandoning your efforts.

On Day 109 of a 280-day weight loss effort that I closely monitored, I had my first binge. Rather than ignore it, however, I decided to look at binge eating and understand what was behind that binge and binging in general.

For me, that particular day had been an especially frustrating one. I was working hard on an article assignment. My editor had called and left a message that he needed me to call him back to discuss my assignment. He left his home number. I called him back and his mother-in-law answered. She told me she was taking all the calls because my editor's wife had just left for the hospital and was about to have a baby.

I was embarrassed because I didn't know this, and I felt I had been put into a position that made me look like a totally self-absorbed person whose only concern was her assignment. But I didn't even know my editor's wife was pregnant, let alone that she was having her baby at the very time I was calling about my assignment. Furthermore, the editor set it up by leaving his home phone number rather than leaving an office number, so I could get his voice mail and have him return the call at his convenience.

I'm sure it's hard for anyone else to see why this situation seemed upsetting enough to me to cause me to binge for the first time in 109 days on a weight management program. But it did, and I did.

The only way I stopped the binge from becoming a pattern again was to understand, without passing judgment on the feelings or myself, how I was feeling, and why.

"You went to the food because the food was there," my therapist explained. "You open up the refrigerator and it's there."

When I eat, *I'm* in control, I realized. I can select, or reject, a specific food, or decide even if I will eat at all.

Not so in real life. Not being able to talk to my editor when I needed him—not feeling in control—led me to falter in my weight-loss program and take control of the only thing I could: food.

I felt somewhat less compelled to continue the binge and the compulsive overeating after I gained some insight into my motivation by discussing the incident with my therapist. Instead of continuing the bingeing, I only had a 130-calorie ice milk bar before going to sleep.

I looked up bingeing in some of the books I have about obesity. In *Such a Pretty Face: Being Fat in America* by sociologist Marcia Millman, there is a chapter entitled "Compulsion and Control in Eating". She quotes some of the women she interviewed on the "out of control" experience of bingeing. Then she insightfully writes:

> It is important to note here the irony that eating is something used in the spirit of *asserting oneself* against an outside force or power (and therefore, asserting personal control) at the same time that eating is recognized as being inconsistent with the person's own recognition of what is good for herself. That is, eating may be an act of self-assertion and selfpreservation against outside forces that are annihilating.

If you have a history of bingeing, try to figure out what is behind it for you. What coping strategies have you developed for your occasional binges that will help you to reach your goal? Will you go for food choices that are less likely to sabotage your efforts—vegetables versus huge quantities of fattening desserts? Are you working with a therapist or eating disorder expert who is helping you understand what is behind your binges? Are you distracting yourself with other activities besides bingeing and overeating until the urge to binge has passed?

Purging as a way of coping with bingeing is not a healthy response to bingeing; that way of coping leads to the eating disorder of bulimia, which has severe health consequences and can, in some cases, even be fatal. If you are dealing with bingeing in this manner, get yourself help, so you can deal with it in a more positive way.

Continue Setting Realistic Goals

My time management research has led me to know this truism: a little bit of pressure is motivating; too much tends to shut someone down. It is useful to your success to keep yourself interested in your creative weight management program, but you will have to be patient with your progress.

You will reach your goal by motivating yourself but avoid becoming overly concerned so that you don't have unrealistic expectations.

Losing 1–2 pounds a week sounds very minimal, but if you multiply it by just four weeks or even five months, you could safely and easily lose $4 \times 2 = 8$ pounds or $20 \times 2 = 40$ pounds that way.

Crash diets are dangerous; furthermore, the changes may not even be permanent; there is usually a rebound effect, as short-term deprivation cannot be sustained.

If You Fall Off the Wagon, Get Right Back On!

Just as it took longer than a day to become overweight or obese, it is going to take more than falling off the wagon for just one meal or even one day to completely sabotage your efforts.

The problem is that when someone who is trying to change her or his weight has a bad day, he or she may say, "What's the difference! I might as well eat!" and she or he ends up consuming more food, and doing more damage to the weight program than the original "cheating". It's not the one piece of cake you had that you weren't planning on having—it's the three or four additional pieces, the candy bars, the ice cream, or the second or third portion of the main course or desserts in response to that little bit of cheating.

Resist throwing in the towel because you went off your program.

It's the total week that will count when you have your weekly weigh-in, rather than just one meal.

That is the key difference between a creative weight management program that has the potential of helping you transform your eating and exercise habits and attitudes in a permanent, positive way, and all the other times you have dieted. Since you are doing this for the rest of your life, you do not have to dwell on the few times you overeat or are unable to follow the program.

Furthermore, by developing more insight into perfectionism and realizing how it is a fantasy as well as another way to make yourself feel bad about yourself, you can give up the myth of perfectionism since you are focused on feeling good about yourself whatever your weight or shape.

"I couldn't stop eating chocolate over the weekend," I confided to another weight watcher.

The woman seemed relieved that I had shared that with her, since by looking at my shape, which was close to my goal weight by now, she had assumed that I no longer had any "pulls" toward compulsive overeating.

The difference was, however, that when I regained my control, I began a new "Day One" rather than letting my overeating of high caloric chocolate become a binge of two, three, or more days with the subsequent regaining of some or all of the weight I had lost.

Instead, I geared back up, went right back to being conscientious about what I was eating and was able to keep on losing weight.

Vacations happen. Special occasions happen. There are mood swings. There are a myriad of reasons behind losing control and overeating that may cause you to find it harder some days to stay on your program than other days.

But if you keep following your program, and getting back on it if you have a brief lapse, you will, eventually, find yourself reaching the numerical goal you have set for yourself.

It will happen.

Staying the Course

Beginning a weight loss and maintenance program with a positive attitude and the firm commitment that *this time* it will be different is very challenging. *This time* you will keep up your weight loss program, even if you get discouraged after a few hours, days, weeks, or maybe even months. *This time* you will approach special occasions and holidays with the attitude that you can get through those activities, especially those involving food—and how many of those activities do involve food and drinking—without gaining an enormous amount of weight.

All these statements sound good in theory, but are a lot harder to put into practice. It is rare to find someone who says that losing weight and keeping it off is "easy". So how do you keep yourself motivated and on track?

Whatever healthy program you follow will probably work for you if you stick to it. How do you stick to it? A 55-year-old Massachusetts-based woman who wants to lose 50 pounds shared when asked what she wants to learn about weight management: "How to keep the motivational voice in my head from going silent".

In Chapter 5, "Getting Started," I shared 15 ways to motivate yourself to find the time to start a creative weight management program. Review those 15 ways.

Now also consider how you are keeping up your motivation to continue on your creative weight management program until you reach your goal. What ways work for you to motivate yourself to continue with any goal that takes time?

Reward yourself as you lose the next smaller unit of weight out of the total you have to lose, no matter how small, or as you get into the next size clothes.

Here are some additional techniques that help to reinforce working toward a goal, whether it is losing weight and keeping it off, getting a good grade on a test, or writing a report that gets your boss to notice what an excellent job you're doing:

Fifteen Ways to Reinforce Your Motivation

1. Make a list of the physical improvements since you have taken off some weight, whether that means finding it easier to walk up the stairs, or feeling more energetic. Review your list to reinforce the benefits of keeping up your weight loss efforts.
2. Take out your "before" picture. Take a new picture of how you look now. Compare the results.
3. Refer back to the list of reasons that you wrote down in Chapter 5, "Getting Started", for initially wanting to reach your preferred weight. Review that list to reinforce your original motivations.
4. If you are following a weight program that includes attendance at weekly meetings, or working one-on-one with a nutritionist or weight counselor, seeking help from your leader, counselor, or others who are part of the self-help group you are participating in, may help you stay motivated.
5. Try the reward system. Make the commitment to yourself for a reward if you continue toward your preferred weight whether that includes going on vacation, buying a new wardrobe, getting orchestra seats to a live performance, or

whatever you value as a reward.

6. Make a list of the reasons you want to continue on your creative weight management program until you reach, and maintain, your preferred weight:
7. Consider what has happened over the time you have been on your creative weight management program. Can you find one or more positive experiences that happened because you were feeling better about your appearance? Focus on those benefits so far, and remind yourself that they occurred because of your efforts.
8. If you used to write down everything you ate but you have stopped keeping track lately, go back to tracking each and every thing you are eating, including when and why you are eating them.
9. Review the health benefits of reaching your preferred weight, and remind yourself that your hard work and discipline are worth it, since you are lowering your risk of heart disease, certain types of cancer, diabetes, and increasing your longevity, for starters.
10. Remind yourself that you deserve to feel positive about how you look and the clothes you wear.
11. Are there any goals that you have achieved in your school, work, or personal life that did not take hard work and effort? Reinforce how good it felt to achieve those goals and how good it is going to feel when you reach your preferred weight, and maintain it.
12. Write down some of the comments you've been hearing about yourself since you are following this creative weight management program. Put those sayings on a bulletin board over your desk or write them in your daily appointment book, or keep those compliments stored in your electronic assistant, and reread those comments as often as necessary.
13. Read articles, books or watch movies that reinforce the social, career, and health benefits of getting to your preferred

weight and staying there.

14. If you have been pursuing your weight loss on your own, try asking a family member or friend to join you in your efforts. It might help you to become recommitted to your weight loss and maintenance goals, as well as your exercise regimen.

Washington, D.C.-based Mary Moslander shared with me that she has first-hand experience with daily communications with her friend, Janice, that Mary sees as the key reason she was able to lose, and keep off, the 30 pounds that she still needed to lose after delivering her third daughter.

Her daily conversations with Janice, between 9 and 10 each morning, started out focusing on what they were each eating, but it soon evolved into something more. As Mary explains:

> "Over time, the conversations were less and less about our motivation and coping strategies and more about the things we enjoyed talking about. [But] If you know you're going to have a conversation with someone, it causes you to think about it more: 'What *did* I eat yesterday?'"

Even if daily phone, e-mail, or in-person conversations with a friend is more frequent than you want for yourself, like Mary and Janice's example and the numerous other examples of friends or family members helping each other to achieve their fitness goals, e.g., there are other options, including eating healthier, working out together at the gym, or participating in a regular sport activity, such as tennis. The positive power of helping each other with our weight and exercise goals is clear.

Be careful, however, to evaluate if this suggestion helps or hinders your efforts since some family members or friends, through no fault of their own, may not be ready to deal with their own weight challenges, or may actual deter your efforts because issues of competition or jealousy become a factor.

15. If you are bored with the program you have been following, or are at a plateau for an inordinately long period of time, cautiously consider switching to a new medically sound, supervised program. It might help to motivate you to keep going until you reach, and then can maintain, your goal. But before you pursue this possible option, work hard with those supervising your current weight loss efforts to analyze what you are eating and how much exercise you are doing to see if there might be a way to adjust your current plan, so you can see the results you want, or you can decrease the boredom of staying on the same plan.

Remind Yourself of All the Non-weight Related Achievements in Your Life

This might be an excellent time to reinforce the key concept behind *The Fast Track Guide to Losing Weight and Keeping It Off*: You have been successful in so many areas of your life, you can succeed at losing weight and maintaining your preferred weight just as you figured out what you needed to do to achieve in other school, career, or social situations, and did it.

What are your achievements that you need to remind yourself of as you continue on your path to your preferred weight and exercise regimen? Take a few moments to write those achievements down. Fill in the blanks below trying to write down at least two or three achievements in each of the key areas.

School achievements

1. ______________________________.
2. ______________________________.

3. ____.
4. ____.
5. ____.

Career achievements

1. ____.
2. ____.
3. ____.
4. ____.
5. ____.

Social accomplishments

1. ____.
2. ____.
3. ____.
4. ____.
5. ____.

Coping Strategies

Here are some additional strategies that may help you as you continue reinforcing your new healthy eating habits, exercise routines, and continuing your creative weight management program until you reach your preferred weight:

1. **Sharing food:** Whether you're eating at home or eating out, try sharing your portions with someone else if what you are served is either too high in calories or too big a portion. For example, I wanted to have a frozen pizza the other day, but I knew the entire serving for one would be too much for that meal. I asked my husband if he wanted to share it for lunch, and we did.

   When you eat out, some restaurants even have a fee

built in that enables you to officially share a portion without feeling as if you're doing something sneaky.

Or if you feel self-conscious asking to share a plate or a portion at the restaurant, you can always leave half the meal and ask to take the leftovers home for yourself later on or for another family member.

2. **Leftovers:** What a concept! Not just when you are eating out, but also when you prepare food at home, you do not have to eat everything on your plate. You can leave some of the food, storing the leftovers in the refrigerator for another meal or freezing the leftovers for later use. You can alter the leftovers by reusing it in another dish, so you avoid the possible boredom of eating the same foods too often. Make sure you follow safe guidelines for storing and reusing any prepared foods. You could even consider throwing out the extra food if you know you are unlikely to want to eat it as part of another meal or snack.
3. **Vary your menu:** Be careful about having the same foods day after day. From boredom can come the need to snack on tastier, less familiar foods. Do you remember the days when eating just one or two very plain foods was considered the way to lose weight/diet? Fortunately, the newer and more enlightened thinking is that you do not have to deprive yourself, or eat just one or two "healthy" foods, to lose weight and reach your preferred weight goal. Almost every food, as long as you know how to count it in the program you are following, is allowed. Vary your main courses, as well as the vegetables, fruits, condiments, and desserts that you prepare and consume.
4. **Delegate cooking:** Just as delegating at work helps you to focus your energies on the tasks and jobs that you do best, delegating cooking may help you to have fewer pressures and temptations in the kitchen. Not everyone is able to hire a personal chef, but there are other affordable options. You can

delegate to other family members who may actually enjoy having the opportunity to cook or bake now and then. You can delegate to take-out food. More and more supermarkets offer take-out. Of course, there's always the traditional take-out from a restaurant. You can also consider buying pre-packaged foods, if your food plan permits it, whether refrigerated, canned, or frozen, that could be considered as delegated cooking.

5. **Lead a balanced life:** Research reported in *Shape* magazine by Kathleen Doheny based on an *International Journal of Obesity* study found that working more than 40 hours a week increased the likelihood of putting on pounds in the 7,000 women studied. The 25 per cent who had gained weight the previous year "were more likely to work overtime, report job fatigue or have difficulty combining work and family life".
6. **Get enough sleep:** According to a study in the journal *Sleep*, adults between the ages of 32 and 49 who slept less than seven hours a night were more likely to be overweight or obese than those who slept more than seven hours.
7. **Get on the scale regularly for information and feedback:** Keeping track of what you weigh as well as your weight loss is also useful information. Even if it's tough to get on the scale that first time, that's an important first step to helping you face reality. But remember that the number on the scale is just a number. It reflects how many pounds you weigh, not whether or not you're a good person or if you have self-control or even if you are a success or a failure. It provides information for you to work with, nothing more, and nothing less. Once you have your starting point of what weight you weigh when you begin your weight loss and maintenance journey, it will then tell you if you are losing weight, staying the same, or gaining weight. It offers feedback to your eating and exercise efforts.
8. **Save time by using prepared foods and adapting those**

foods to your program: Here are some suggestions to use canned, frozen, or otherwise prepared convenience foods in more creative ways to increase the usefulness of those products in your weight program:

- Extend the prepared canned or frozen meal by adding frozen, fresh, or canned vegetables to the dish, such as green beans, asparagus, cauliflower, broccoli, or any other preferred non-starchy vegetable. It will fill you up more.
- Once you've cooked the canned or frozen food product according to the directions on the package, take the meal out of the container and put it on a regular or paper plate rather than eating it out of the original container. Taking the time to serve the prepared food in a more festive way will help you to feel better about what you are eating, and yourself.
- If your family is having a meal that you prefer not to taste because you feel you might lose control, try to match it up with a canned or frozen food product that you feel more comfortable eating because the prepared food is in a specific portion, such as lasagna, spaghetti and meatballs, or macaroni and cheese.
- Go for variety in canned or frozen prepared foods. Even if you have a couple of favorites, try to vary your selections to help avoid the boredom.
- You don't have to eat the whole thing, nor do you have to use the canned or frozen food product as your entire meal. Use half of it as an appetizer and put the rest away or share it with a friend or family member, such as pizza or pasta.
- Build a meal around the canned or frozen food product by adding a salad, additional vegetables, beverages, even if only water, and dessert.
- Put a lot of time and energy into creating an exciting and inviting table. Select a tablecloth, dishes, knick-knacks,

fresh flowers, and other visually stimulating additions to the table so your meal is more festive and appealing.

- Eat sitting down, even if you're having your canned or frozen food product alone for lunch or dinner. Avoid eating standing up at the counter.
- Tell your friends and family members about your favorite canned or frozen food products. Share about which ones you like the most, just as you would share about favorite recipes. It's a way to spread the word about these delicious, convenient, and healthy meals, a time-saving and useful alternative to take-out or cooking from scratch.
- Visit the website for canned or frozen food products, if the manufacturer has one. Hopefully at their website you will find lots of useful information about weight issues as well as recipes.

11

FINDING TIME TO EXERCISE

Creative Weight Management Principle #7:

Include exercise, and non-food stress reducers, such as meditating or keeping a journal, into each day.

What do you think of when someone mentions the word *exercise*? A man with sweat pouring off his arms and chest as he completes the tenth mile of a daily run? Waking up at 5 a.m., and swimming fifty laps a day at the local health club? Doing twenty-five push-ups or having a one-hour daily regimen at the gym? Running five miles at 6 p.m. after work?

Sure. Those are all examples of exercise. But it's not what you *have* to do, especially when you first start your weight control efforts and you have not exercised in a very long time. To start getting some of the benefits of exercise as an aid in your creative weight management program, you simply add movement (exercise) to your daily activities.

First and foremost, you have to be concerned with your safety, so do not do anything that might put you in harm's way. But if it is safe to do so, start your new exercise regimen, as I did when I was still overweight: by parking your car a few blocks from your destination and walking or running the extra distance to your destination.

If you take the subway or a bus, get off one or two stops before your regular stop or walk a couple of stops before your stop, and then take the subway or bus to your office. For example, in the last few weeks, a friend of mine who lives in Manhattan and her neighbor have started walking 30 blocks to the subway—or over a mile—rather than getting on at the nearest stop, and then taking the subway to work. She lives 62 blocks from her office. They now start each day with a walking workout that gives them extra energy to get through the workday as it burns up calories.

Instead of just letting the dog out in the backyard, take your dog for a long walk, or just walk or run up the road or around the block, asking a family member, neighbor, or friend to join you on a regular basis. Even housework, especially washing the floors and using the vacuum, can be a form of exercise. If you have stairs in your home, go up and down the stairs, as if you are on a stair machine at the health club. Put on a CD or radio, and dance. One of my favorite songs to dance/work out to is by the group Eiffel 65. It's the ninth track of the Eiffel 65 CD and it's got the words "Move Your Body" in it. It's hard for me to listen to that song without starting to dance, aka exercising. Or turn on the TV and work out to Denise Austin's exercise show or on other workout shows on network or cable stations. You could also use any of Richard Simmons' workout videotapes, such as "Dance Your Pants Off"! Join a local team, get involved in tennis, or start a participant sports activity of your own, such as volleyball.

Why Exercise?

Exercise burns up calories. Exercise makes you feel good, both while you're doing it and right after you've finished. Exercise usually means being away from the refrigerator and food. Exercise may decrease depression. Exercise may decrease the possibility of getting cancer, and it may help those with cancer in their recovery.

- Exercise improves the quality of life.
- Exercise prolongs life.

- Exercising in the older years reduces the chances of getting dementia by 30 to 40 per cent.

So, in order to "find the time" to exercise, you have to do with exercise what you're doing with following a weight reduction (and once you're at your ideal weight, a weight maintenance) plan: make exercise a priority. You have to commit to the benefits of exercising, convince yourself that it will make you feel and look better, and burn up calories, and that it is a priority in your life.

In order to make finding time to exercise a priority for you, take a few moments to write down why it's important for you to exercise. Your reasons may be the same, or differ, from the generalized reasons.

Write down at least three reasons why it is important for *you* to exercise:

1. ______________________________.
2. ______________________________.
3. ______________________________.

Once you accept that it is paramount to your overall self-improvement and weight management plan to exercise, your next step indeed is to find the time.

Eating Less, and Exercising More,
Is Key to Losing Weight and Keeping it Off

This concept, as hard as it is to accept, has been documented through scientific and anecdotal research. If you want to read just two documents supporting this thesis, see "Managing Your Weight", a booklet from the American Heart Association (Dallas, Texas) or the article "95% Regain Lost Weight. Or Do They?" by Jane Fritsch, published in *The New York Times*, 25 May 1999, page F7.

The Debate over Moderate Vs. Rigorous Exercise

Until recently, it was thought that moderate exercise—using up 2,000 calories or more a week through sports, climbing stairs, or walking—could prolong life. This was based on a 1986 study of some Harvard University men which found that such moderate exercise led to death rates one-four to one-third lower than for men who were less active.

But a 1995 study of 17,300 Harvard University alumni indicated that it is hard or vigorous exercise, not moderate or light exercise, which is necessary to see a reduction in death rates.

What is vigorous or hard exercise? According to *The Journal of the American Medical Association*, as adapted by Jane E. Brody in her *New York Times* article, "Trying to Reconcile Exercise Findings, here are examples of vigorous exercise (defined as activities that raise oxygen consumption to more than six times the level burned by the body at rest):

- Walking briskly uphill or with a load, 4–5 miles an hour for 45 minutes a day, 5 times a week.
- Fast cycling or racing, more than 10 miles an hour, 1 hour, 4 times a week.
- Swimming (fast treading or crawl); doing laps 3 hours a week.
- Cardiovascular exercise (stair-climbing machine or ski machine), 2 to 3 hours a week.
- Racket sports (single tennis or racquetball), an hour of singles tennis three days a week.
- Fishing (wading in a rushing stream).
- Canoeing (more than 4 miles an hour).
- Moving furniture (picking up heavy furniture).
- Mowing the lawn (using a hand mower).

There are other benefits to exercising: weight-bearing exercises, such as lifting weights, help increase bone density, which can offset the onset of osteoporosis, a condition that means literally "porous bones", which afflicts 50+ women and leads to a hunched appearance or an increase in debilitating broken bones.

Exercise Benefits a Child's Mind

Based on a study by The Society for Psychophysiology Research reported in *Health Science* magazine in an article entitled "Exercise Benefits Children's Minds", it was found that children who regularly exercise score higher on standardized tests.

According to the article, children who were more physically active had faster reaction time on behavioral tasks, as well as higher scores on the Illinois Standard Achievement Test. What children tend to exercise more? The fit ones. Overweight or obese children exercise less than their fit counterparts in the same way that fit adults are more likely to exercise than those who are overweight or obese.

Exercise Resistance

So why are so many reluctant to exercise or work out?

If you took a poll of why men and women you know don't exercise, most would probably say, "I don't have the time." Of course, there may be other reasons behind that admission, but at least consciously lacking enough time to exercise seems to be the reason for avoiding it. It's more socially acceptable to say, "I don't have time to exercise" than to say, "I hate exercise. I like sitting and watching TV. I like being inactive. I'd like to exercise, but I can't get myself to do it."

Finding the Hidden Time in Your Day to Exercise

In *Creative Time Management for the New Millennium*, one of the most popular concepts I shared is the idea that most of us have "hidden time" in our day that we waste. We could be using that time more productively.

I suggest you apply that concept to your day so you can facilitate your weight loss and maintenance, especially finding hidden time to exercise—whether that means going to the health club before or after work, or during the day, walking or running, taking up an active sport like tennis, squash, or swimming, or the myriad of other ways to exercise. Make sure you check with your physician and get a check-up and clean bill of health before embarking on an exercise program, especially if you've been sedentary and inactive for a long time, whether or not you are moderately or severely overweight.

It's true. You *are* busy! There's work to be concerned with, as well as family, community, and even pet obligations. Somehow those 24 hours in a day get filled up, day after day. Have you done what you wanted to do each and every day? Perhaps you got the work done and cleaned the kitchen, but you didn't read a novel or get to exercise.

But that's the concept behind *The Fast Track Guide to Losing Weight and Keeping It Off*'s approach to weight loss and maintenance. Now consider the hidden time in your day when you could fit in 10 or 20 minutes of exercising. If considering the hidden times in your day is an overwhelming consideration—and the idea of exercising daily is too much to handle right now—consider the hidden times in your week, for starters.

Waking up 20 minutes to an hour earlier than you're used to—and before everyone else in the house—is a terrific hidden time that could be used for exercising. When my children were infants, toddlers, and in preschool, I forced myself to get up at 4 a.m. to write so I could keep my career going and still provide childcare without the necessity of a nanny or day-time babysitter.

Even though both my sons are in high school and college

now, I've kept up the habit, having a solid two hours of quiet time for myself since I still wake up early. Although I give myself the luxury of sleeping until 5 a.m., I use those two hours to write, but I could use the time for exercising. Whenever I get to the gym and work out, I am so pleased with the way I feel. If I keep at it, I know daily exercise will become a habit.

A study conducted by John Raglin, Ph.D., an Indiana University research psychologist, discovered that working out with a spouse is an excellent way of ensuring that you will stick with your program. In his study, after a year, 90 per cent of the couples that worked out together were still continuing their exercise routine compared to only 50 per cent of married men and women who were exercising alone. Taking the time to exercise together was motivating them to keep up their programs.

Some couples, especially those with young children who rarely find the time or have the money to get out regularly together on a date, might welcome making the time to exercise together. Some tennis court, especially if it is part of a community center, may offer babysitting services or you could arrange this on your own or consider sharing a sitter, depending upon the age of your infant or child, with another parent or two; it might be possible to double up with another couple with children and take turns exercising and watching the youngsters.

Newsletter editor and publicist Fran Silverman and her husband, who have a grown daughter, work out together daily and have done so throughout their marriage. Their exercise consists of walking, running, lifting weights, or swimming. Silverman, who is 5'8", is at a weight that she is pleased with, 139. "My husband and I are exercise fanatics and have been so for a long time," Silverman explains.

Consider putting an exercise bicycle, a rowing machine, or a treadmill in your family room or bedroom, and get on it as you watch TV, or do it soon after waking up.

Weekends provide additional time to exercise; try to find some time during the work and school week, as well, so you can pace out your workouts more regularly. You actually have to be careful about the weekend workout phenomenon, whereby you are sedentary all week only to exhaust and overwork yourself on either Saturday or Sunday at the health club or jogging in the park. Your body, heart and muscles are not used to such an extensive, intensive workout. The dangers of such an extreme and sudden workout might actually outweigh the benefits.

With exercise, as with most activities, having a plan, a steady plan, will take you further than starting and stopping, or extreme efforts only to be followed by no effort at all.

Use the space below to work out an exercise plan for yourself:

My Exercise Plan

____

____

____

____

____

____

____

____

____

____

Here are some other ways to get yourself to commit the time for exercising.

Make an appointment to exercise and put it in your daily appointment book as if it has the weight of a business or doctor's appointment that you rarely would cancel. If it helps, make an appointment with someone else, commit yourself to working out with your spouse, a friend, or, if you have the funds, a personal trainer.

Call it something besides exercise; call it fun, and just do it. Look over the previous list of vigorous exercises that can make a positive difference in your life expectancy, the majority involves sports, such as single tennis, racquetball, swimming, or bicycle riding. Instead of thinking of it as exercise, think of it as being involved in a sport, or just being active.

Remember those days as a child, those days before being a couch potato became the epidemic it is today, or everyone was spending hours in front of a computer screen on the Internet, when you were always outside riding your bicycle, or on the tennis team at school, just because it was fun? Remember when it wasn't exercise at all but just being active? Go back to those days and that way of thinking!

Combine Working Out with Something Else You Have to Do

Do you have an indoor mall near your home? Do you have shopping to do? Some indoor malls allow walkers to use the mall for exercising for an hour before it is open to the public. So, from 9–10 in the morning, you can walk in the mall. If you need to go shopping, time it so you end your walking regimen by getting a jump-start on the stores.

Another benefit of indoor mall walking is that you can do it throughout the year, creating a reliable routine for yourself. It is not subject to the vicissitudes of the weather, like jogging or bicycle riding, or the cost of joining a health club, or purchasing gym equipment for your home.

Apply Creative Time Management Principles to Exercising

The three main principles of time management include prioritizing, goal setting and goal shifting. If you want to stick to a regular exercise schedule, it has to be a priority.

Every day you'll have to make decisions about what exercise

you're going to do, so you must make a complete commitment to this goal and to the maintenance of it. You have to set goals, and you also have to be sure to review the goals that you've set. Your goals must be realistic since incorporating exercise into your life is not an overnight thing.

The reason so many people stop exercising after they start is because they fail to make maintaining the new habits a priority. You also have to be sure that you really understand the complexities of your resistances to exercise, addressing your own specific problems. In addition, you have to be ready to experience your new, positive feelings in non-food ways. It's scary when you remove the protective "unfit" barrier.

Often people who are sedentary hide themselves, but you should be sure to dress nicely and try out new looks no matter what shape you're in. There's always going to be someone more fit and attractive than you, so you have to accept yourself and not punish yourself. Face the world, no matter what you weigh.

There are so many ways to let exercise into your life. I have friends who go running religiously as a group on Sunday mornings, and then afterwards they have a healthy brunch. Or make walking your mode of transportation instead of driving.

Get active with your family, go bowling, hiking, or play tennis. Run on the treadmill while you watch your favorite TV program.

You must take away the negativity associated with exercising—that it's a burden—and instead focus on how good it makes you feel and how easily you can include it in your everyday life.

Be Kind to Yourself As You Increase Your Exercise Regime

At 204 pounds, I just wanted to get through the day. I was not physically or mentally up for rigorous exercise. As noted before, I started my exercise regimen in a very low-key way, adding more concerted exercise as I lost weight. Now, just three pounds within my goal, I am striving to increase the frequency of my workouts from once or twice a week to every other day. I have also increased the time from 20 to 30 minutes.

So be kind to yourself as you slowly, but surely, make the time to add exercise to your daily activities.

12

TACKLING WEIGHT: A MAN'S PERSPECTIVE

Being overweight, obese, or underweight are conditions that impact men as well as women even if women have been much more visible until now in their efforts to deal with this problem. The hit reality TV show, "The Biggest Loser", has helped the public to see that men, as well as women, are upset with being overweight or obese for health, social, or career reasons. They no longer have to deal with their weight challenges secretly or on their own. They, too, can seek out support from other men and women who are motivated to develop better eating and exercise habits that will help them to achieve their weight and fitness goals.

I asked my husband, Fred, who, like me, has dealt with dramatic weight fluctuations throughout his adult years, to share a male perspective on his weight challenge. In June 2010, he joined Weight Watchers with me; over the next year, between us we lost almost 100 pounds—Fred lost 45 pounds. Here is what Fred wrote at the time of that successful weight loss about his male perspective on the weight challenge:

I had been afraid to get on a scale for nearly a year. I knew I weighed more than I ever weighed before. My clothes no longer fit, and I had just purchased some new suits to replace the ones that stopped fitting many pounds ago. The weight crept on slowly, over time, like a sneak attack. People who hadn't seen me in some time made comments like "You've put a few extra pounds there", "What happened?" or "I see you found the weight I lost". It was embarrassing, to say the least. Embarrassing mainly because the obesity implied to me that I had a weak character, unable to apply the will power needed to stop the gluttony.

There were physical problems too. In the middle of the night, I would wake up with pains in my chest brought on not by a heart attack but a form of gas generated from an overtaxed digestive system.

The decision to do something about this had weighed, pardon the pun, on my mind for weeks before I finally took action. It happened one morning when I could no longer ignore the fact that none of the belts in my closet would fit around my expanded waistline. So I pulled out the scale that had been pushed under a table, dusted it off, and climbed on. I closed my eyes and took a deep breath. When I looked down, I saw a number I had never seen on a scale before. I weighed 282 pounds. I'm six feet, four inches tall, and should weigh between 210-220 pounds.

The number 282 was imprinted on my mind. I could no longer deny the reality that something was very wrong and that if I did not take action, I would probably die. I was slowly eating myself to death.

For a Father's Day present to myself, my wife asked me to join her in starting a weight loss and maintenance program. She was concerned about the health impact of the extra weight on me, and she also thought it would be more fun to follow the program together. I agreed because that's what my wife was committed to doing, but also because I know it's a healthy, flexible, and affordable program. I had four times before joined another program that was much more costly; it also gave out supplements as part of the program as well as a much more restrictive meal plan approach to eating. Three of those four times I was very successful on that diet but at this point, I preferred to share the same diet program as Jan. That made meal planning quite a bit easier, since I had an ally in the battle of the bulge. Somehow having another person going through the tedious process of weighing portions and eating healthy made the process easier to bear.

I've been on the weight reduction plan for a year, and I have lost 50 pounds. Losing the last 20 pounds, however, has become very challenging for me because lately I've been somewhat more casual in my commitment to this challenge.

Getting motivated again to stay with it till I reach my goal is the hardest part. I've been at the same level for about a month now. The only way to recommit to this weight challenge is to convince myself that my life depends on losing that 20 excess pounds that I'm carrying, and you know what? It does, although I am very grateful and pleased that I have already lost 50 pounds.

To lose weight and to keep it off takes a lot of will power, planning, and time management. It's the time management part most people aren't aware of. They know it takes will power and that you have to plan ahead for what you eat. But if you don't manage the time to accomplish this, you're going to return to all the bad habits that got you fat in the first place, grabbing the quick meal, the fast food, the easy donut or candy bar for quick energy.

I can tell you from experience that weight management does not work in the short or long run without time management.

To successfully lose weight and keep it off, there are too many new things you have to do and too many changes in your eating habits you have to alter that all take time. And if you don't make the time in your daily schedule to address these changes, you won't do it.

So if, like me, you apply the time management techniques described in this book, you'll also be more likely to master the difficult, but rewarding, task of weight management.

Some Thoughts about Exercise

One of the cruel realities of keeping the weight off is that without exercise, it may start to creep back on, even without eating any more. It has something to do with metabolism. Your body adjusts to how many calories it takes to keep it running. My problem is that I never seem to have time for exercise. Or so I thought. Actually, my problem was that I never made the time for exercise. So I put some of the time management techniques that I've learned to work on this exercise challenge.

I decided to combine exercise with other activities. One of the best exercises is walking. It's something I have to do anyway. But just walking seemed like a waste of time to me. So I combined walking with reading, or actually listening. Listening to recorded books or music became my new walking partner. Now I can go for a 45-minute walk listening to a book without feeling the time was wasted on merely walking. I call these morning strolls my "power walks" because I feel so powerful when I'm finished.

Facing Travel-related Weight Management Challenges

One of my biggest struggles occurs when I'm traveling, either on a business trip or vacation. Business trips are especially difficult times for me to stay on track. There's some kind of subconscious voice telling me that because I'm traveling, I don't have to pay attention to what I'm eating. Traveling is stressful enough. Why add to it the pressure by eating right?

Well, the simple answer is that if you don't, you're going to pay for it with extra pounds. I can put on 10 pounds on a five-day business trip. It usually takes me three times as long to lose those 10 pounds. I remember putting on 7 pounds at a three-day conference in New Orleans and how it took more than two weeks to take it off.

So now I eat with the knowledge that I'm either going to pay now or later, so that keeps me in reality when I'm traveling. If I follow sensible eating habits on the road, I won't be faced with the job of losing the extra weight when I get home.

Also, most hotels have gyms with treadmills to take power walks with a good book, so I have no excuse not to exercise on these trips either.

It all comes down to putting yourself and your health high on your list of priorities. Once you do that, you'll make the time to do the right thing. Not only will you feel and look better, you'll also be sending a positive message to your family and even your friends and relatives. If they see you're putting your health and weight first, whatever your age or profession, they will have evidence that this is a lifestyle choice and not something to do when you get around to it.

Author's Note: Fred regained a lot of the weight he had lost in the years after writing this essay, but, fortunately, he returned in 2014 to Weight Watchers® and is already down 15 pounds. He is back on the road to achieving lifetime weight control and maintenance, a goal that he is committed to for the long haul. I see Fred as an excellent example of how to get back on track after a relapse rather than completely abandoning the weight loss and maintenance goal just because he didn't keep the weight off.

13

THE LAST 10 POUNDS

This is what happened to me: I'm going along, losing pound after pound, sometimes I go up because of a business trip, vacation, or going back to my old habit of turning to food and overeating when I'm upset, but I keep going and, one day, I'm just 10 pounds from my goal!

I am so eager to get to that finish line that I start skipping breakfast and even try to miss a meal or two to speed up the process. But it backfires! Not only don't I lose more weight, but also I soon discover to my dismay that I actually gained 2 pounds. I am going in the wrong direction! Starving, I am told, shuts down one's metabolism to compensate for the calorie deficit. That is an important factor as to why starving, crash dieting, or eating too little is *not* the healthy or preferred way to lose weight, even if you "only" have 7–10 pounds to go or to lose in the first place. Furthermore, starving or fasting can be dangerous; there can also be a rebound from the deprivation that could lead to bingeing.

After this happened, rather than retreating in isolation, as I am prone to do if I see myself "failing", I decided to talk to my weight loss program facilitator, Mary, about my struggles. Yes, the pull to stay away, and avoid facing the scale, was strong, but I am glad I went there, to face reality about the weight gain and also to try to get some help.

Mary suggested that I do a couple of things to help myself in the last phase of my weight loss—it seems there really is a Last 10 Pound syndrome! First of all, she suggested I increase the amount of water I was drinking, adding three extra glasses.

Second, she suggested I also increase the amount of exercising I was doing. At the time, I was walking on the treadmill once or twice a week for twenty minutes.

Third, she suggested that I really watch what I was eating, making sure I got the amount I was supposed to get each day, not eating too much or, conversely, too little.

Soon after that discussion, I stopped at our local bookstore and purchased a book, *Lose Those Last 10 Pounds*, by exercise guru Denise Austin. Chapter 3, "10 Dos for Losing the Last 10", is especially helpful.

To help me in my own efforts to lose those stubborn last 10 pounds, I had to "stay the course", keep doing what I know works even though I was at a plateau for weeks. But I also went back to writing everything down in a much more rigorous and detailed way. Every morsel counted! I also changed the type of exercise I was doing. Instead of just walking on the treadmill, I added swimming. The very first time I swam ten laps, when I got on the scale the next morning, I had dropped a couple of pounds. The key is to keep going, with your preferred weight clearly in sight, and definitely not overeating or turning to a dependence on food again, just because you are frustrated by your weight efforts.

At a certain point, if you are truly sticking to your program and working out regularly, you may also want to reconsider your preferred weight at some point. Is it realistic for now, or is your body telling you that you have achieved the preferred weight for where you are now?

What I learned is that the last 10 pounds, like the first 10, are extremely tough. It has given me a new appreciation for those who want to lose "only" 10. I will never think of it as "only" 10 ever again. Those 10 are going to be challenging to take off and keep off, but you are not afraid of a challenge or you would not have gotten this far along on your path.

Recommit to your preferred weight goal and tackle each and every last pound with the commitment and enthusiasm that you approached the first 5 or 10 pounds that you wanted to lose. You *can* do it!

What Will Happen When You Reach Your Preferred Weight or Goal?

Whether it is two weeks, a month, several months, or a year or more after you started your creative weight management program, the day finally comes and you reach your preferred weight. If you are following a formal program, there are systematic ways to acknowledge and reward the achievement of your goal weight. If you are working with a nutritionist or physician, or another supervised program, how reaching your preferred weight is handled may vary from person to person, and from plan to plan. If there is no formal reward system in place for making your preferred weight, make surc you reward yourself. Buy a new outfit, call up everyone you know who is supportive of your weight challenge and share the good news, plan a vacation that you've put off for several months or years, call a friend who lives far away and do not pay attention to how long you are on the phone.

What are you going to do to mark the occasion of reaching your preferred weight?

When I reach my preferred weight I will:_______________

In addition to the reward you will give to yourself, or others will bestow on you, when you reach your preferred or goal weight, you may also want to reexamine your own fears or fantasies about what this will mean. You probably did this early on in this book and/or in your program, but it may be weeks, months, or even a year or two later, depending upon how much weight you had to lose, as well as other factors. Now is an excellent time to re-explore those concerns as you reach your preferred or goal weight.

What do you think will happen differently because you are at your preferred weight? What will be the same?

If you were using your weight as an excuse not to do something, it is important to reexamine that situation now, with your end (new beginning) in sight. If it is still hard to make cold calls for your business, losing weight is not going to make that easier. If you were questioning whether or not you had the money or the time to go back to graduate school, losing weight may not be the reason you now feel the timing is right. If your social life has improved because you are no longer obese, you may want to reconsider some of the career or educational goals you had if you now want to put your time to use in ways you could not have envisioned 10, 20, 50, 100, or more pounds ago.

Depending upon how much weight you had to lose and how long you were overweight or obese, along with how long your transformation has taken, your expectations for yourself because of your weight loss may not be borne out by the reality of achieving that preferred weight goal.

But for starters, once you achieve your preferred or goal weight, it is time to put into practice the eighth creative weight management principle: reapply the first seven principles, so that you make "maintaining my preferred weight" your new priority. Some help with maintaining your weight loss is the subject of the next chapter.

14

MAINTAINING YOUR PREFERRED WEIGHT

Creative Weight Management Principle #8:

When you reach your preferred weight, make maintaining your weight loss your new #1 priority. (If you ever regain even 2 pounds, go back to principles 1–7 to get back to your preferred weight.)

Ask any celebrity what's harder: the climb to the top or staying at the top? Most will answer, "Staying at the top".

The climb is exciting.

The climb has others cheering you on. There are changes, often dramatic ones if you're losing weight, especially large amounts—25, 50, 75, 100, 200 pounds—but once you get to your goal weight, you will pretty much continue to look the same.

Everyone, including you, will get used to the "new" you.

You achieve your preferred weight. Now, what do you do?

Since this book is about a lifetime creative weight management program, you need to approach the attainment of your weight loss as just one step in the process of lifetime creative weight management.

Once you achieve your weight goal, it is time to set a new goal: maintaining your preferred weight.

In that way, creative weight management principle #8 becomes a pivotal principle that can help you to *finally* succeed in overcoming your weight challenges.

For some, once you achieve your preferred weight, there may be a pull backwards:

- To your old habits.
- To your old "you".

What's behind this pull?

It's the resistance to staying at that goal weight that concerns me. What is it about reaching a goal that's so frightening? Why would the fact of no longer needing to lose weight actually seem like a disappointment when compared to the excitement and frenzy of staying with a program?

I thought about this pull backwards, and I thought about how I was feeling when I had previously reached my goal weight. Most important of all, I thought about the times that I could only maintain my weight loss for a few days or weeks.

There was an incredible feeling of emptiness those other times when I reached my goal weight. I felt so empty and I didn't understand that feeling so I tried to get rid of the emptiness by eating. I started eating and it was almost as if someone had taken their finger out of the dam that was being held back just by that one finger.

And I would eat and eat and eat.

And still I felt empty.

This time, I had worked very hard to fill my life and myself up, so when I reached my goal weight, I did not feel empty.

And when I feel that sensation coming back, I remind myself it's emotional, and that I will have to fill myself from within, not with large quantities of food that are beyond what my body actually needs.

Coping Once You're There

This chapter, on maintaining your goal weight, may be the most important chapter in this book for you. That is because very few share the reality of what it means to reach a goal and the possibility that there might be overwhelming or even negative feelings about being thin since it is supposed to be seen only as a positive event.

Of course reaching your goal weight is a milestone. That's what you've been working towards all these days, weeks, months, or perhaps even years. Reaching your goal is a plus. By now, you're looking slimmer, probably feeling a whole lot more energetic and healthy, having higher selfesteem, and happy to be wearing a smaller size.

So, why is reaching your goal such a pivotal time in your creative weight management journey? Because once you reach your goal, you need to adhere to your new, improved eating habits or you will find the weight coming back on, and sometimes at an astonishingly fast rate.

Few learn how to maintain their weight by gradually increasing how much they are eating, so that they can 1) stop losing weight, and 2) find out just how much they can eat without gaining again. This will be discussed in the next chapter.

The problem with reaching a goal is that very few are prepared to deal with all the issues that striving to maintain that goal presents. There is energy and an excitement about having a goal; reaching it is another story. Especially if weight loss is accomplished in a group situation, where each 1–2 pound loss is cheered, once you reach your goal, ironically, the cheering stops. Of course you are cheered for your accomplishment, and fitting into the size you've always dreamed of and looking the way you've always wanted to look are certainly rewards as well, but if you got used to your week-by-week loss as an inducement to stay on a diet, achieving your goal and no longer having that weekly incentive may be disconcerting.

Furthermore, losing weight is the only loss that is seen as a positive in our lives. When we lose a loved one, we feel grief. When we lose money, we feel upset. When we lose momentum, we want to regain it.

Yet we consider losing weight a positive thing.

It is a positive thing, but we need acknowledgement as a powerful force to regain it.

To help yourself deal with the wonderful accomplishment of reaching your goal weight, consider how you felt when you achieved other goals in your life. Did you feel good about it? Did you feel sad? Disappointed? Let down? What did you do next, related to that goal? Did you continue whatever effort was required to reach that goal, or go on to other concerns and let your accomplishments languish?

Maintaining your weight loss is as important (or more important) as reaching your goal.

You reach your goal in a moment; you have to maintain it over a lifetime.

Consider the last goal you accomplished, besides losing weight, and write down that goal on a piece of paper, in your journal, or on the computer or handheld electronic organizer.

How did you feel when you accomplished it? Write those feelings down as well.

Has accomplishing something ever made you sad, or are you always happy over your achievements?

I wrote the poem below when I was actually 2 pounds under the goal I had initially set for myself, but 5 pounds above the goal I now want. The numbers are somewhat different from my most recent—and hopefully my last—major weight loss—I started out at 213 that time instead of 202.2—as well as the time frame—it's taken a year and a half instead of just nine months—but the message of the poem is the same:

A Number on the Scale

I stood on the scale this morning and cried,
It read, "135".

Not that 213 was not great
It's just that I did not need
all that extra weight.

It has been a nine-month journey,
I have lost 78 pounds
But look at what I've gained—
    self-confidence
        self-esteem
            self-control
And the ability to look the mirror square in the eye,
again.

I am proud of what I have accomplished.
I am proud of what I have done
But I know that losing the weight
Is only the start of the fun.

The most fun will emerge
As my new self stays slim and trim

As I now begin to hear an unfamiliar—and untrue—refrain, "But, my dear, you're getting too thin!"

This is what I have learned, the hard way, about reaching your goal: the only way to keep that goal is to set a new one. The new goal should be: keep off the weight and maintain that weight loss. Everyone says maintaining the weight loss is the hardest thing to do. They always tell you that when you're on the diet, however! When you're on the weight loss diet, you have to consider getting the weight off. But you have to consider maintenance all the way along, even the very first moment you begin your weight loss program.

By the same token, maintenance is part of reaching your goal. As noted before, creative weight management has five pivotal steps:

Step 1–Getting motivated to start a healthier eating and exercise/weight loss and maintenance program.

Step 2–Day One: Starting your program.

Step 3–Continuing your program.

Step 4–Reaching your preferred weight or goal weight.

Step 5–Maintaining your preferred weight through healthy eating and exercise.

I remember how painful it was when I had finally lost the weight a few years back and I met a friend for coffee. She took one look at my thinner self and made a snide comment about how often I'd lost weight only to regain it. In a tone of voice that was not caring or kind, she wanted me to defend myself and explain to her how I was going to ensure that I kept the weight off "this time". I have not spoken to her since. I used to think about the joy I would feel if I ran into her and I had still kept the weight off, but now I feel strong in the knowledge that I am a valuable person, whatever my weight, and I need to surround myself with friends who are supportive about the weight challenge I deal with every day.

Your weight loss and maintenance is key to you. No one should be making you feel self-conscious about what you are achieving, whether this is the first, second, fifth, tenth, or fiftieth time you have tried to lose weight, and keep it off.

Your "After" Picture

Date ____________

You might want to reinforce your accomplishment by putting an "after" picture in your journal or adding it to this book. Remember that every day is actually Day One, but reaching your preferred weight and staying there is a milestone in your journey.

Taking a Relationship Inventory

Taking a relationship inventory can be helpful. Who is kind and helpful to you in your weight loss and maintenance challenge? I am certainly not advocating that everyone cut off contact with anyone who says or does something that is perceived as non-supportive during or after a weight loss program. If the person who is not supportive about your weight challenges is someone you want to continue to be with, whether it is a spouse, child, sibling, parent, friend, or extended family member, or have to be with, such as a coworker, boss, employee, or business associate, how can you react to him or her in a way that helps you? Can you try to educate that person about how painful his or her comments are, and why you would appreciate it if the topic is avoided or if words are chosen more carefully? Or you may choose to ignore the comment and chalk it up to insensitivity.

No One's Perfect: What If You Relapse?

What I've learned over the years is that any sound, healthy diet will work if you stick to it, so the key is sticking with it.

Weight loss, and maintenance, is complicated and perplexing, however. If it was just a question of taking off the weight, there are few of us who would have a weight problem. For me, I've observed, and research and statistics verify, that for most it's keeping it off that's even harder.

Saying that "the old habits return" is too easy, too simple an answer.

It's deeper than that.

I have been working on getting a deeper insight into compulsive overeating and bingeing.

If you have limitations because of underlying psychological issues that you need to deal with, getting professional help may be what's needed to help you avoid the yo-yo syndrome. In contrast, if your pull back is just because of becoming too lax about what you are eating or about how much exercise you are doing, becoming part of a formal maintenance plan may help you reinforce your new healthier habits. In that way, you will learn, through a maintenance plan, how to apply the same creative weight management determination that you applied to your initial weight loss. Keeping your weight off, and continuing to exercise, becomes the new goal.

As most anyone with a weight challenge will tell you, it is pretty easy to put on 5, 10, or even 20 pounds in a relatively short period of time if you are out of control and unaware of what you are putting in your mouth.

A woman I met had shared that she had gained three pounds after a vacation with some family members. Rather than hide from that reality of a 3-pound gain, she went back on her weight loss program, even staying to hear the program explained so she would have her renewed efforts reinforced.

In researching this book, I interviewed Carol, who at that time was a 38-year-old single technology recruiter who had lost 39 pounds. Her Last Straw to motivate her to take control of her weight was when her family physician asked her, "Do you want me to give you the same medication in your thirties that your grandmother is taking?" Carol's family has a genetic predisposition to heart disease, high blood pressure and cancer, so keeping her weight within a normal range is at least one way she could positive contribute to a healthier and longer life for herself.

Besides, Carol adds, "I was sick of people saying 'You're too pretty to be big', or, 'You're too pretty to be fat'."

Carol was always somewhat overweight, but when she moved from her home state to another one a couple of hours away by car or train, after college, and her mother was no longer preparing food for her, the pounds piled on. She explains some of the reasons why: "Going out, drinking a lot, no sleep, going out and going to the diner at three or four in the morning for a full breakfast, then getting up and eating lunch with my friends."

She chose to lose the weight very slowly because it had to fit into her demanding lifestyle, which includes a great deal of socializing and entertaining related to her job. She lost it and kept it off for several years. But four months ago, several injuries occurred simultaneously that prevented Carol from the daily strenuous exercise workouts that were helping her to burn up calories and keep her weight down. That, combined with a vacation with her niece and nephew where she decided not to be vigilant about what she was eating, led to a 10-pound weight gain.

But she is committed to getting the extra 10 pounds off. Tomorrow is her Day One. She's kept off 30 pounds and she's going to get off that 10 she regained. "I've lost and gained weight for years," Carol explains. "But this time, this is it. I'm done. No more going back."

Taking charge and losing those 10 pounds, and keeping those pounds off, are a priority now. It was making her new healthy eating habits a priority that got her to her preferred weight initially and she knows it will get her there again. "I bring my lunch to work," Carol says. "It's pre-planned. I measure. Unless I have a work event, my food is preplanned. On Sundays I cook and bake, and I freeze. There's no window of opportunity for me to say there is anything in my house to eat that isn't pre-cut, pre-bagged. I have no excuse to have to get something to eat, ever. That's purely by design. I will let myself go on Sundays. I treat myself to French fries."

Author's note: A while after I initially interviewed Carol, she relapsed and gained back a lot of the weight that she lost. But the good news is that Carol is back to her program, taking the weight off again, a pound or 2 a week, rather than denying her situation and facing a lifetime of being overweight or obese.

Carol is just one weight loss, maintenance, relapse, and renewed weight loss story. Each and every one of us with a weight challenge will have a unique weight loss and maintenance and, as you have seen from my story shared at various points throughout this book, many of us have a myriad of stories at different times in our lives. But the key concern is that you are striving to reach, and maintain, a healthy weight for your frame, height, and activity level, and that you are focused on eating healthy, enjoying food, not misusing it for emotional eating or denying its pleasurable aspects, as well as engaging in an exercise program that is right for you taking into account your age, medical condition, health, weight and lifestyle.

Here are some tips for getting back on track if you have regained any weight that you wanted to lose and keep off, including if you are still on your weight loss journey to your preferred weight:

10 Tips for Restarting After You Regain Extra Weight

1. If you can get back on track before you completely regain all the weight you lost, it will be that much easier, and take that much less time, to get yourself back to your goal weight. The key is to do something about your weight, regardless of how much you regain.
2. For whatever reason you want to try a new approach to dieting, that's fine. As long as your new way is healthy, supervised, affordable, and you see results, go for it. Don't return to the diet you were following when you initially lost your weight out of a misguided sense of loyalty to that program or that diet. If you think it could work for you again, fine. Go back to it, but if you want to start a new

plan, that's okay too.

3. See this new diet as a new beginning. If you kept off some or even most of all the weight you initially lost, that's great. But you are starting fresh, from this new point, and you need to see this as a new effort.
4. Go back to the chapters in this book that deal with starting a diet. It doesn't matter that you relapsed and you're starting again. You are starting, so put the emphasis on that.
5. Put into practice once again the eight principles of creative weight management that you learned in this book.
6. Make reaching and maintaining your goal weight your new #1 priority.
7. Planning is key to success in your weight loss as well as your weight maintenance success. Plan your day, plan your meals, plan what you'll buy at the store, plan what you'll do when you eat out, and plan how you'll handle special occasions, like parties or big events.
8. Congratulate yourself for facing the scale and starting again.
9. If you have to buy one or two items in your wardrobe to get you through this transition time, let yourself do that. You can donate those items as soon as you get back into your preferred smaller wardrobe.
10. Re-evaluate your goal weight to make sure you pick a realistic one if that is one of the factors behind your relapse and weight gain.

Most of all, congratulate and reward yourself for getting back on track and not burying your head in the sand. It's your body; it's your life.

15

SPREADING THE WORD

You've done it! You have lost the weight and kept it off, and now you feel committed and enthusiastic about helping others deal with their weight challenges.

The tricky part, however, is that your well-intentioned excitement and zeal may actually backfire, pushing those you love and care about away, and actually hurting, rather than helping them, to get and stay motivated.

For example, recently my mother has been bringing up the fact that my husband has to lose a lot of weight. I've (foolishly, perhaps) shared her concerns with my husband.

Finally, he wisely said to me: "Please be patient with me. I was patient with you."

If others granted you the opportunity to discover on your own that you needed to, and could, do something about your weight challenge, whether it necessitated getting over or dealing with emotional eating, eating disorders, or lack of exercise, you need to grant others the luxury of self-discovery as well.

Nagging can not only turn people off, but it can also really be a source of trauma and pain. Here are some suggestions for more positive ways than nagging to inspire others to want to change:

- Wait to be asked for help rather than volunteering it in a pushy and unwelcome way.
- Belittling someone, name-calling, pointing out someone's overweight or obese is cruel, especially since you were there once. Instead, be understanding and compassionate about how hard it is to have a weight challenge.

- Just as others had to wait until you were ready to deal with your weight challenge, you have to wait for others to be ready.
- It is okay to share about how much better you feel on any and all levels since you have lost weight, if you do it in a compassionate and caring manner rather than a bragging or insensitive way.

Becoming a Role Model for Others

One of the benefits of learning a new healthier way of eating and seeing the pounds melt away because of positive changes and eating the foods you like (within your plan) is you become a role model to yourself and to others. You embody the fact that being the weight you want does not require deprivation. It is, instead, based on a new positive attitude towards food, exercise and yourself.

My goal in writing *The Fast Track Guide to Losing Weight and Keeping It Off* was, and still is, to help motivate others to achieve what I have accomplished. It is not just the number on the scale or the size I now fit into; it's my increased confidence and energy level. It's my ability to exercise regularly because it now feels good, as well as actually being good for me.

I take my role of motivating others very seriously. It is also crucial to reinforce how pivotal being motivated is. Today more than ever in our information-laden world, having the facts or knowledge is rarely the reason someone cannot accomplish something today, especially if she or he knows what to do. Helping someone to want to do it is a whole other question, one that is even more complicated.

But a woman I will call Jessica who needs to lose 50 pounds simplified that challenge for me in my weight history survey, which asked this question: "What would you like to learn about weight management?"

Her reply: "How to motivate myself."

Motivating her, and you, is my goal.

I am spreading the word that it is possible to lose weight and keep it off. It is possible, even though for some of us it is more challenging than it is for others. But I am spreading the word to adults, teens and children that the benefits of eating healthy and regular exercise outweigh the sacrifices and new ways of approaching food and exercise that are necessary for this transformation.

If you have succeeded in achieving your weight goals—which may also include developing or reinforcing a positive body image, whatever your weight, shape, or size—learning how to spread the word of your accomplishment in a way that inspires and motivates, rather than shutting down and turning off, is a gift. You have received the gift of loving yourself and how you look—maybe for the first time in your life if you had unrealistic standards that no one, including you, could achieve—which will empower you forever.

Help me to spread the word about the inner beauty that comes from self-love, compassion, empathy, mentoring others, and setting a positive example of maintaining a healthy weight and regular exercise regimen.

As psychiatrist Thomas Szasz wrote in *The Second Sin*:

> Men often treat others worse than they treat themselves, but they rarely treat anyone better. It is the height of folly to expect consideration and decency from a person who mistreats himself.

16

AFTERWORD

I know that I smoked my last cigarette on 22 December 1984. Smoking is over for me. I've never smoked another cigarette.

Yes, if I'm in a smoke-filled room I experience a craving for a cigarette, and I go through a "mini-withdrawal", but I also know that, for me, to have even one cigarette would mean to be back to 3-1/2 packs in no time.

Of course, it's hard to quit smoking. Just ask any current smoker who wishes he or she could quit.

But you can live without cigarettes.

You can't live without food.

Food is always there, and so, for me, my weight problem will always be a challenge. That's probably one of the biggest "ah-has" in this weight loss and maintenance journey for me. The realization that I'm a foodaholic and that my challenge with food is not something that I will ever be cured of. I can at least control it though, and have my weight within a healthy and manageable range.

I have courageously gone public with my up-and-down weight challenges but without the shame and embarrassment that too often is associated with "falling off the diet wagon". I am not hiding until I am a size 7 again. I have a lot to share; my research and insights need to start helping others today, not tomorrow.

Good luck with your own weight challenge!

Ironically, it is *because* my weight loss success has not been in a straight line—there have been ups and downs and setbacks, but finally I am at peace, not at war, with food—I am a role model because it has not been simple or easy for me to achieve this weight loss and to gain positive self-esteem. My current weight loss success, and my lifetime weight loss and maintenance struggle, is real and probably far more common than someone who has weight to lose, does it, and never again has to cope with the challenge. With many Americans gaining 10–25 pounds during the holiday period, between Thanksgiving, Chanukah or Christmas, and 1 January (New Year), dealing with weight issues has become an annual concern.

Here, in summary form, are the eight principles of creative weight management:

1. Figure out *why* you're overweight and overeating.
2. Prioritize this weight loss and maintenance effort. Commit to it wholeheartedly.
3. Get a medical check-up and select a medically sound, supervised plan that you will follow.
4. Plan, shop, and prepare for each meal.
5. Keep track of everything you eat or drink every day.
6. Create manageable smaller, interim steps or goals.
7. Exercise regularly (as long as you have your physician's approval to do so).
8. When you reach your preferred weight, make keeping it off your new priority. If you ever regain even 2 pounds, go back to principles 1–7.

I hope the principles of *The Fast Track Guide to Losing Weight and Keeping It Off* help you as you apply them to your weight challenge, the same way that the creative time management principles have been successfully applied to overcoming other self-defeating habits, like procrastination, perfectionism, disorganization, and doing too much at once.

Of course there are some who find losing weight and keeping it off not that big a deal. Or perhaps you were like that at another time in your life, perhaps when you were younger, or even a few years ago, if you were more active or you were working full-time and not home as much with food nearby tempting you all the time.

For most, losing weight and keeping it off is a very tough, demanding challenge. As noted before, it is not something you can achieve once and for all. It is a constant challenge especially if you turn to food in times of joy, stress, sadness, frustration, happiness, pressure, or just when in social or business/entertaining situations. It is all too easy to find "creeping obesity" transform your trim figure into the next size and then the next.

Staying in reality by getting on the scale may help to at least keep any weight gain manageable. By the same token, you want to be careful to monitor that you are not losing too much weight. If you need to go to the next size in clothes, that's a warning sign. If possible, try to put the principles of creative weight management back into practice again so you catch yourself after going up just one size, or having to go to the next notch on your belt.

Prioritizing your weight challenge is empowering, and it is more likely to get you the results you want just as it will help in your school or career goals. Make losing weight and keeping it off, as well as adding the appropriate amount of exercising, key concerns in your life. Your longevity, and the quality of your life, depends on it. Don't wait until it's hard to walk up the stairs, or your doctor gets test results that cause her or him to warn you, "Lose weight, or else."

Chocolate, cake, a lollipop: these are not "bad" foods. It's how much you consume, and also, when and why. My goal for you: that reading *The Fast Track Guide to Losing Weight and Keeping It Off* helps you to become an epicurean who is also fit and satisfied.

I hear parents brag that they do not have any "fattening" foods in their house even though their children or teens crave those foods. Then they tell the tales, always greeted with laughter, about how a child, or spouse, "sneaks in" the "bad" food, but it is treated as a temporary situation that will soon be replaced with the "good" kitchen cupboards with only "good" foods.

Unfortunately what that parent or spouse may not realize is that she or he is unwittingly passing on his or her own dysfunctional approach to food and eating. Control is being seen as something outside oneself rather than from within.

Join Us in Our Determined Efforts to Deal with Overweight People, Obesity and Eating Disorders

Let's fight the growing epidemic of being overweight, obese, and eating disorders together! You are not alone in your battle. Take comfort in knowing that there are others, so many others, including me, who fight this battle every day. The good news is that, like me, you can win the battle and reduce the lifetime fear that you will gain, or regain, any weight you lose, and you will not know why.

An estimated 300,000 Americans are dying annually because of illnesses related to being overweight and obese; countless others internationally are also dying because of weight-related afflictions, including the increased risk of heart disease and diabetes because of excess weight, putting extra burdens on themselves and their families, as well as those healthcare systems. But even one death because of being overweight or obese is too many, since being overweight or obese are preventable, and curable, health challenges.

It is not just in the US that being overweight or obese are rising. According to the World Health Organization (WHO), internationally 22 million children under the age of five are reported to be overweight. The website of the WHO, at its regional office for the Western Pacific, begins its overview on the topic of obesity with this telling sentence: "The prevalence of overweight people and obesity is increasing worldwide at an alarming rate." The powerful statements continue: "Both developed and developing countries are affected."

Changing for the Better

This book is the culmination of the years I have spent to *finally* achieve a healthier attitude towards food. I now embrace food as a wonderful part of life. By and large, I no longer misuse it or deprive myself! In moderation, and depending upon either the portion of the food or the choices I make within a particular cuisine, I enjoy all kinds of food, including pizza and pasta, Chinese, Thai, German, and Japanese food, ice cream cones, cheesecake, and even candy. I've discovered the wonder of "portion control" as well as the pride of creating and serving tasty, nutritious meals for my husband, our sons, when they join us for a meal, since they are now grown up and on their own, and myself. I'm in control of food! I'm not battling it as much nor am I depriving (or overindulging) myself except now and then, and then, but without self-loathing, I catch myself and get right back on track.

This is the gift I have given myself that I want to give to you through the insights and techniques I have been sharing in *The Fast Track Guide to Losing Weight and Keeping It Off*:

> I've been obese.
> I've been overweight.
> I've been at my goal weight.
> I feel and look better when I am within the healthy weight range for my height and frame.

But, as noted before, it is essential to love yourself, whatever you weigh, but that does not mean you cannot forge ahead towards a healthier weight.

Please also note that advocating that you become, and maintain, a recommended weight for your height, body type, and activity level, does not mean becoming so obsessed with thinness that you never feel thin enough. The goal of a healthy attitude toward food and maintaining an ideal weight does not diminish recognizing and treating those with the grave problems of anorexia nervosa or bulimia, whereby the quest for thinness has led to severe eating disorders, including starvation or eating followed by regurgitating, that left untreated could even be fatal.

Have faith and fresh hope that you *can* and *will* succeed at becoming and maintaining the weight you want to be!

I applaud your decision to do something about your excess weight! Bravo to you in your efforts!

Congratulations for giving yourself and your family the gift of a healthier approach to food, weight and exercise.

Thank you for sharing your journey with me. I hope this book proves to be a catalyst to positive, permanent change in your eating habits as well as your approach to your weight challenge. It is my hope that this book proves useful to you and that it inspires you as I cheer you on from the sidelines.

You probably know quite a lot already about food, eating, cooking, weight loss, exercise, and related subjects. I recommend that you become as much of an expert as you can on yourself—the motivations behind your overeating, the pattern to your eating habits, what food program will work best for you so you can lose weight slowly and keep it off, what foods may trigger a binge, if you are prone to bingeing, and anything else about food, being overweight, and obesity that will help you in your journey.

The good news is that food manufacturers are starting to respond to the health needs of their customers. For example, I recently purchased a bag of light potato chips. The manufacturer had reduced the calorie count in one serving—17 potato chips—from 175 calories to just 70 calories. It is easier than ever before to find single portions of practically everything you might like to eat, or individual servings that are "just" 100 calories, making it somewhat easier to "stop" yourself from eating the entire bag of peanuts, or pretzels, or cookies.

So not only can you have your cake—within limits—and eat it too, you can have your potato chips as well! And it's okay if you cannot stop at eating just one, as long as you try to stop at eating 17 (or, if you eat 34, you make sure you keep track of how many chips you have consumed).

It may have taken me half my lifetime to achieve this goal, but I am so happy that I am at this place of peace with food and I have the rest of my years to enjoy it: I am in control of what I eat and when I eat it. The food is not good or bad and it does not control me. I make those choices, and I reap the benefits or the consequences of those choices. How I wish I had reached all these wonderful insights and this state of being in control of my eating and my food 25 years ago. But, fortunately, I still have lots of terrific years ahead of me, years that I have helped to improve by giving myself more stamina and a healthier weight and size, not to mention dressing in brighter and more attention-getting clothes once again, now that I am not self-conscious of being overweight.

Whatever your age, and whether you have 5, 10, 25, 50, 100, or more pounds to lose (or you need to gain weight or develop a healthy body image and regular exercise regimen)—or perhaps you have achieved the weight you want and you just want to maintain it—you are not alone in your challenges. I am there for you. There are eating disorder experts, therapists, nutritionists, weight loss program leaders, self-help groups, and, of course, family and friends who are also cheering you on.

Viva chocolate (in moderation)!

Finally, try to have fun while you lose weight and keep it off. There is definitely a benefit to knowing you are doing something that will provide you with a better life, a healthier life, even a longer life, and that you do not have to deprive yourself of tasty foods just to lose weight and stay within your preferred weight.

Finally, *bon appétit,* as we all pursue the Greek ideal of a sound mind and a sound body!

APPENDIX

Eight Principles of Creative Weight Management*

1. Figure out why you're overweight and/or overeating.
2. *Prioritize* doing something about your weight and eating habits as your #1 concern.
3. Get a medical check-up and pick a medically sound, supervised plan to follow.
4. Be prepared. Plan, shop, and prepare for each meal or snack.
5. Keep track of what you're eating or snacking on or drinking every day.
6. Create more manageable goals, reward yourself as you go down the scale, as you lose the next smaller unit of weight of the total you have to lose, such as each 1, 3, 5, or 10 pound loss.
7. Include exercise, and non-food stress reducers, such as keeping a journal or meditating, into each day.
8. When you reach your preferred or goal weight, make maintaining your weight loss your new #1 priority and goal.

---

*Reprinted from *The Fast Track Guide to Losing Weight and Keeping It Off* by Jan Yager, Ph.D. (Hannacroix Creek Books, Inc., 2016, available in e-book, print, or audiobook formats). Permission granted to print, post, or share these principles as long as credit is given to the author and to her book; and nothing is edited, deleted, or added to these principles.

BIBLIOGRAPHY

Abelson, Reed. "F Is for Americans Getting Fatter." *New York Times.* "Prescriptions" (The business of Health Care), July 7, 2011, Posted at http://www.prescriptions.blogs.nytimes.com

Alexander, Linda Lewis, Ph.D., R.N., C. and Judith H. LaRosa, Ph.D., R.N. *New Dimensions in Women's Health*. Boston, MA: Jones and Bartlett Publishers, 1994.

Amen, Daniel F. *The Amen Solution*. New York: Crown, 2011.

Austin, Denise. *Lose Those Last 10 Pounds*. NY: Broadway Books, 2001.

Baar, Karen. "Time for a Fitness Pyramid? Extra Benefits from Exercise at Any Age." *The New York Times*, March 29, 1995, p. C1, C6.

Bailey, Covert. *The New Fit-or-Fat*. Foreword by George Sheehan, M.D. Boston, MA: Houghton Mifflin, 1977, 1978, 1991.

__________. *Smart Exercise: Burning Fat, Getting Fit*. Boston: Houghton Mifflin, 1994.

Baker, Russell and William Zinsser, eds. *Inventing the Truth: The Art and Craft of Memoir*. Boston, MA: Houghton Mifflin, 1998.

Barkas, J. L. (a/k/a Jan Yager) *Meatless Cooking: Celebrity Style*. NY: Arco, 1978. (Originally published at *The Meatless Celebrity Cookbook*, 1975, NY: Grove Press.)

__________. *The Vegetable Passion: A History of the Vegetarian State of Mind.* NY: Scribner's, 1975. (With a new introduction, audiobook, available through www.audible.com, 2014)

Benson, Herbert, M.D. and Eileen M. Stuart, R.N., C., M.S. *The Wellness Book.* NY: Fireside, 1992.

Brody, Jane. "Personal Health: Just How Perilous Can 25 Extra Pounds Be?" *The New York Times*, September 20, 1995, p. C1.

__________. "Trying to Reconcile Exercise Findings." *New York Times*, Sunday April 23, 1995, p. 22.

Brownell, K.D. "Obesity and Weight Control: The Good and Bad of

Dieting." *Nutrition Today*, 1987: 22 (3), 4-9.

Campos, Paul. *The Obesity Myth.* New York: Gotham, 2004.

Chernin, Kim. *The Obsession: Reflections on the Tyranny of Slenderness.* NY: Harper & Row, 1982.

Chou, Jane Shiyen. "Better Way to Exercise." *Family Circle*, September 1, 1995, p. 44.

DeSalvo, Louise A. *Writing as a Way of Healing.* Boston, MA: Beacon Press, 2000.

Doress-Worters, Paula B. and Diana Laskin Siegalin cooperation with the Boston Women's Health Book Collective. *The New Ourselves, Growing Older.* 2nd edition. NY: Simon & Schuster Inc., 1994, 1987.

Downie, Chris. *The Spark: The 28-Day Breakthrough Plan for Losing Weight, Getting Fit, and Transforming Your Life.* Carlsbad, CA: Hay House, 2011.

Ernsberger, P. and P. Hasker. "Rethinking Obesity: An Alternative View of its Health Implications." *The Journal of Obesity and Weight Regulation,* 1987: 6, 58-137.

Gelles, David. "A C.E.O.'s Management by Mantra." *New York Times,* March 1, 2015, pages BU1, 6.

Goodrick, G.K. and J.P. Foreyt. "The Business of Weight Loss: Why Treatments for Obesity Don't Last." *Journal of the American Dietetic Association,* 1991: 91, pp. 1243-1247.

Guiliano, Mireille. *French Women Don't Get Fat.* NY: Knopf, 2005.

Harcombe, Zoe. *The Obesity Epidemic: What Caused It? How Can We Stop It?* Monmouthshire, UK: Columbus Publishing Ltd., 2010.

Heatherton, T.F. and R. F. Baumeister. "Binge Eating as Escape from Self-Awareness." *Psychological Bulletin* (1991), 110, pp. 86-108.

Hirschman, Jane R. and Carol H. Munter. *When Women Stop Hurting Their Bodies.* NY: Fawcett Columbine, 1995.

Hollis, Judi, Ph.D. *Fat and Furious: Women and Food Obsession.* NY: Ballantine Books, 1994.

Kolata, Gina. "Catching Obesity From Friends May Not Be So Easy." *New York Times,* http://www.nytimes, August 9, 2011.

Lilley, Ray. "TV Time a Big Predictor of Obesity in Children, New

Zealand Study Says." The America's Intelligence Wire, September 30, 2005.

"Lower stress and sufficient sleep aid. Weight loss." *Environmental Nutrition* July 2011: 8. *Student Edition*. Web. 22 Aug. 2011.

Mackenzie, Natalie Gingerich. "Get-Slim Gadgets." *Self* May 2011: 109. *Student Edition*. Web. 22 Aug. 2011.

Maine, Margo. *Father Hunger: Fathers, Daughters & Food.* Preface by Craig Johnson, Ph.D. Carlsbad, CA: Gurze Books, 1991.

Manson, JoAnn E., M.D.; Walter C. Willett, M.D.; Meir J. Stampfer, M.D.; Graham A. Colditz, M.B., B.S.; David J. Hunter, M.B., B.S.; Susan E. Hankinson, Sc.D.; Chalres H. Hennekens, M.D. and Frank E. Speizer, M.D. "Body Weight and Mortality Among Women." *New England Journal of Medicine*, September 14, 1995, vol. 333, no. 1, pp. 677-724.

McKay, Matthew and Patrick Fanning. *Self-Esteem*. 3rd edition. Oakland, CA: New Harbinger Publications, 2000.

_________ and Catharine Sutker. *The Self-Esteem Guided Journal.* Oakland, CA: New Harbinger Publications, Inc., 2005.

McGrath, Linda. *Set Free: A Woman's Victory Over Eating Disorders.* Tokyo & New York: Japan Publications, 1992.

Middleton, Laura E., Ph.D., et. Al. "Activity Energy Expenditure and Incident Cognitive Impairment in Older Adults." *Archives of Internal Medicine*, Vol. 171, No. 14, July 25, 2011, pages 1251-1257.

Moriyama, Naomi. *Japanese Women Don't Get Old or Fat.* NY: Delacorte, 2005.

Pierre, Colleen. "Preventing Obesity Can Become a Full-Time Job." *The Advocate*, May 17, 1995, p. C3.

"Obese kids." *Manila Bulletin* 21 Aug. 2011. *iCONN Custom Newspapers - International Newspapers*. Web. 22 Aug. 2011.

O'Connor, Anahad. "Meditation for a Good Night's Sleep." *New York Times*, February 24, 2015, page D4.

Ogden, Cynthia L., Ph.D.; Margaret D. Carroll, MSPH; Brian K. Kit, M.D., MPH; and Katherine M. Fiegal, Ph.D. "Prevalence of Childhood and Adult Obesity in the United States, 2011-2012. *Journal of American Medical Association (JAMA)*, February 26,

2014, Vol. 311, No. 8, posted at jama.jamanetwork.com

Olivy, J. and C.P. Herman. *Breaking the Diet Habit: The Natural Weight Alternative.* NY: Basic Books, 1983.

O'Neill, Molly. "After Thigh Master, a Stream of Fitness Gadgets." *The New York Times*, March 29, 1995, p. C1, C6.

Pfanner, Eric. "Hazards Lurk Between TV and Sofa." http://www.nytimes.com, August 22, 2011.

Reynolds, Gretchen. "A New Placebo for Exercise." *New York Times*, November 25, 2014, page D6.

_________. "How Exercise Can Keep the Brain Fit." *New York Times*, http://well.blogs.nytimes.com, July 27, 2011.

Roth, Geneen. *Breaking Free from Emotional Eating.* NY: Penguin Group, 2003.

Ryan, Donna H., M.D., et.al. "Nonsurgical Weight Loss for Extreme Obesity in Primary Care Settings." *Archives of Internal Medicine*, Vol. 170, No. 2, January 25, 2010, pages 146-154.

Seid, Roberta Pollack. *Never Too Thin: Why Women Are at War With Their Bodies.* NY: Prentice-Hall, 1989.

Shimizu, M., & Pelham. B. W. "The unconscious cost of good fortune: Implicit and explicit self-esteem, positive life events, and health." *Health Psychology, 23,* 101-105 (2004).

Snyderman, Nancy L., M.D. and Margaret Blackstone. *Dr. Nancy Snyderman's Guide to Good Health.* New York: William Morrow, 1996.

Strom, Stephanie. "McDonald's Alters Happy Meals and Shrinks Fries." http://prescriptions.blogs.nytimes.com, July 26, 2011.

U.S. News & World Report. "Top-Rated Diets Overall." http://health.usnews.com/best-diet/best-overall-diets, accessed 8/22/2011

U.S. Preventive Services Task Force. *Guide to Clinical Preventive Services,* 2nd ed. Baltimore, MD: Williams & Wilkins, 1996.

Wolf, Naomi. *The Beauty Myth.* NY: William Morrow, 1991.

Wooley, S.C. and D.M. Garner. "Obesity Treatment: The High Cost of False Hope." *Journal of the American Dietetic Association* (1991), 91, pp. 1248-1251.

Yager, Jan, Ph.D. *365 Daily Affirmations for Creative Weight Management.*

Stamford, CT: Hannacroix Creek Books, Inc., 2002.

___________. *365 Daily Affirmations for Happiness.* Stamford, CT: Hannacroix Creek Books, 2011.

___________. *365 Daily Affirmations for Time Management.* Stamford, CT: Hannacroix Creek Books, 2011.

___________. *Creative Time Management.* Englewood Cliffs, N.J.: Prentice Hall Inc., 1984.

___________. *Creative Time Management for the New Millennium.* Stamford, CT: Hannacroix Creek Books, Inc., 1999.

___________. "Creative Weight Management: An Audio Book." Stamford, CT: Hannacroix Creek Books, Inc., 2000.

___________. "Meatless Diet: Meal Planning." Minneapolis, MN: Lakewood Publications, Inc., 1980.

___________. *Put More Time on Your Side.* Stamford, CT: Hannacroix Creek Books, Inc., 2014.

___________. *Productive Relationships: 57 Strategies for Building Stronger Business Connections.* Stamford, CT: Hannacroix Creek Books, Inc., 2011.

___________. *The Pretty One.* Stamford, CT: Hannacroix Creek Books, Inc., 2011.

___________. *The Time to Lose Journal.* Stamford, CT: Hannacroix Creek Books, Inc., 2000.

___________. *When Friendship Hurts.* NY: Simon & Schuster, Inc., Touchstone Books, 2002. E-book edition, 2010. Audio edition, Brilliance Audio, 2012.

___________. *Work Less, Do More*, 2nd edition. Stamford, CT: Hannacroix Creek Books, 2012. (1st edition, Sterling Publishing, 2008.)

Zied, Elisa with Ruth Winter. *So What Can I Eat?!* Hoboken, NJ: Wiley, 2006.